Name _____

Date _____

Venue _____

Course leader _____

First published in Great Britain in 2023

Society for Promoting Christian Knowledge
36 Causton Street
London SW1P 4ST
www.spck.org.uk

British Library Cataloguing-in-Publication Data
A catalogue record for this book is available from the British Library

ISBN 978–0–281–08921–5

1 3 5 7 9 10 8 6 4 2

Typeset by Fakenham Prepress Solutions, Fakenham, Norfolk NR21 8NL
First printed in Great Britain by Ashford Colour Press

Produced on paper from sustainable sources

BREAD OF LIFE

The Christian life through the lens of the
Eucharist

GUEST BOOK

Contents

List of illustrations

Foreword

Dear Guest

It is with a real sense of joy that I welcome you to *Bread of Life*. This course is offered to the Church by the oldest of the Anglo-Catholic devotional societies, the Confraternity of the Blessed Sacrament. Because of the Covid pandemic, it has taken something like four years to see this course come together, and my time as the CBS Superior-General has just come to an end. However, it still remains for me to commend this to you in the hope that it will help you to discover afresh how central is the Eucharist to our faith. Through it we celebrate the enduring presence of Jesus Christ in the way that he promised us. That presence is a transforming one as we travel with him on our pilgrim journey. Every time we break the Bread together as he asked us, as did those disciples on the Emmaus Road, our hearts burn within us, and we recognize and know him as the Risen Lord of the Church. In this way we, like them, are strengthened and sent out to tell others of the good news that we know in ourselves, that Jesus Christ is indeed the *Bread of Life*!

May this be so for you as well. May *Bread of Life* be a blessing to you on your own Christian journey. We are fellow travellers, on pilgrimage together in the loving company of our ever-present Lord who nourishes us with food he himself gives, his Body and his Blood.

Bishop Roger Jupp

Introduction to the course

Welcome to *Bread of Life*, a course designed from the ground up to be the start of an amazing journey in getting to know Jesus Christ with a new and deeper understanding.

A number of people have come together from across the Church to create a library of teaching resources to help you bring your faith to life. To start with, these resources include this Guest Book and accompanying videos and podcasts on <breadoflifecourse.co.uk>. As you read through the book, there are icons to show you when to click on these on the website.

You can find recordings of the Main talks of the initial six modules, along with PowerPoint slides and other teaching resources, on the website too. These offer useful focus points on key topics and relevant images to help you explore. If you're leading the course, do make use of the deeper theological background material provided to help you prepare to teach each module.

Bread of Life is designed for those taking their first steps towards Jesus, for those who stand firm in their faith and are exploring a greater understanding of that faith, and for those who simply want to understand their desire to reach out and learn more about *something* that they can't quite put their finger on.

As we develop more *Bread of Life* material, we would love to hear from you. What works well? What didn't quite work? What inspired you most? At the end of each session, we'll remind you to give us feedback. We really do want to hear from you. Stories of unexpected insights, of faith found, of shared love . . . anything that you'd like to tell us.

In love, and with prayer for your discovery of Jesus in this course,

Fr. Matthew Cashmore SSC
Chair of the Editorial Board, *Bread of Life*

Bread of life liturgies

At the beginning of a module

Leader   Jesus says:
I am the living bread
which has come down from heaven.
Anyone who eats this bread
will live for ever.

All   **Lord, give us this bread always.**

Leader   As they were eating, Jesus took some bread
and, when he had said the blessing,
broke it and gave it to them.
'Take it,' he said. 'This is my body.'
Then he took the cup
and, when he had returned thanks,
he gave it to them, and all drank from it,
and he said to them, 'This is my blood,
the blood of the covenant,
which is to be poured out for many.
(This is) The Word of the Lord.'

All   **Thanks be to God.**

Leader   Lord Jesus Christ,
in the most wonderful Sacrament of the
Eucharist you have left us the memorial of
your passion;

deepen our reverence
for the mystery of your body and blood,
that we experience within us
the fruit of your redemption.
Who live and reign for ever and ever.

All   **Amen.**

At the end of a module

At the end of an evening module

Leader   On the Emmaus road, they said to him:
Stay with us, Lord, because it is almost
      evening,
and the day is nearly over.
And so he went in to stay with them.
At table he took bread, blessed and broke it,
and gave it to them.
And their eyes were opened and they
      recognized him.

All   **Lord, abide with us also.**
Let our hearts burn within us.

Leader   Support us, O Lord,
all the day long of this troublous life,
until the shadows lengthen and the evening
      comes,
the busy world is hushed,
the fever of life is over,
and our work done.

Then, Lord, in your mercy
grant us a safe lodging,
a holy rest, and peace at the last;
through Christ our Lord.

All   **Amen.**

At the end of a module at any time of day

Leader   Jesus, bread of life:
All   **Feed us now and evermore.**
Leader   Jesus, bread come down from heaven:
All   **Feed us now and evermore.**

Leader   The bread you give, O God,
is Christ's flesh for the life of the world;
the cup of his blood
is your covenant for our salvation.
Grant that we who worship Christ
in the holy mystery of the Eucharist
may reverence him in the needy of this world
by lives poured out for the sake of that
      kingdom
where he lives and reigns for ever and ever.

All   **Amen.**

Leader   Let us bless the Lord.
All   **Thanks be to God.**

MODULE 1

1

I am the bread of life

Aim of this module

This module introduces the Eucharist as the central sacrament of the Christian life by looking at its history, its meaning and its importance to the contemporary Church.

Way into this module

 Begin with the **liturgy** on p. 1

Watch the **video** at <www.breadoflifecourse.co.uk /jerusalem>

The video is set in Jerusalem and explores the **history** of the Eucharist and how it came about from the context of Jesus' ministry and the early Church. The Main talk, following, aims to help us understand the **meaning** of the Eucharist.

Main talk

((꜀)) Also available as a **podcast** at <www.breadoflifecourse .co.uk/maintalk1>

You may, like me, have been brought up as an Anglican. I went to my local church every Sunday, and it was distinctly Low Church. After Sunday School, I joined the choir and I soon became familiar with the tradition of singing hymns which is so much a part of Christian worship. When I was confirmed at the age of 13, I began to receive Holy

Communion once or twice a month, but soon began to feel this ought to be happening more often. I realized I was unsettled because I was eager to do what the service set before me, 'Take and eat this in remembrance that Christ died for thee', feeding on him in my heart 'by faith with thanksgiving'. When a school friend invited me to visit the Anglo-Catholic church he attended, I was immediately caught up by the Sunday-by-Sunday eucharistic worship and knew that this was where my hunger would be fed. Very soon I became a server, which gave me the privilege of being able to watch closely the drama of the altar. And this observation, together with the hymns I learned to sing, taught me the deeper meaning of what was happening and of the mystery into which I was entering. One hymn especially spoke to me: it was 'Alleluia! sing to Jesus!', and through it I felt I knew heaven on earth.

> Alleluia! sing to Jesus!
> His the sceptre, His the throne.
> Alleluia! his the triumph,
> His the victory alone.
> Hark! the songs of peaceful Zion
> thunder like a mighty flood.
> Jesus out of every nation
> has redeemed us by His blood.

Over time, I began to realize that, during the Eucharist, as well as being taken by Christ our Great High Priest through the Temple veil and into the heavenly Holy of Holies, I was also with him at Calvary, kneeling beneath his cross of sacrifice. The hymn 'Soul of my Saviour' taught me to translate that emotional awareness into prayer, and I gradually learned to experience and celebrate the real presence of Jesus in the Blessed Sacrament and to love him more because I yearned to feed on the one who called himself 'the bread of life'.

> Soul of my Saviour, sanctify my breast,
> Body of Christ, be Thou my saving guest,
> Blood of my Saviour, bathe me in Thy tide,
> wash me with water flowing from Thy side.

Why is the Eucharist so important?

From the beginning, the celebration of the Eucharist was the common experience of the first Christians. In their worship, it was what made them different from the rest of the Jewish community. St Luke tells us that the disciples 'devoted themselves to the apostles' teaching and the fellowship, to the breaking of bread and the prayers' (Acts 2.42). While continuing to attend the Temple, Christians were daily 'breaking bread in their homes' (2.46), because this was what the Lord did on the night when he was betrayed. St Paul is the first to witness to this:

> For I received from the Lord what I also delivered to you, that the Lord Jesus on the night when he was betrayed took bread, and when he had given thanks, he broke it, and said, 'This is my body which is for you. Do this in remembrance of me.' In the same way also he took the cup, after supper, saying, 'This cup is the new

covenant in my blood. Do this, as often as you drink it, in remembrance of me.'
(1 Corinthians 11.23–25)

We must take what Jesus did at the Last Supper alongside what the risen Lord did at Emmaus, an action which enabled the dispirited disciples to recognize and experience his real presence with them: having 'broken open' the Scriptures, Jesus took, blessed (i.e. gave thanks), broke and gave the bread at the meal to which he was invited. These actions of Christ are repeated at every Eucharist to help us understand that it is the supreme memorial of Christ. Fulfilling his command, we not only re-enact the Last Supper, we also re-enact (or, perhaps better, *re-present*) what Christ did by his dying and rising. We enter into his sacrifice and join in offering the gift of himself – to the Father, for the world – made once and for all upon the cross. This offering of Jesus was a perfect thanksgiving to God. The Greek word for 'giving thanks' gives us our word **Eucharist**. The Church continues the tradition handed on from the first disciples. Their distinctive practice from the very beginning is ours and sets us apart in the same way.

This act of remembrance is a memorial, but *not* in the sense that the Cenotaph in London is a memorial to those fallen in battle. For the Jew, the Passover meal was a memorial action which made real for them *in the present* that great and enduring act of salvation *of the past* – the escape of their ancestors from Egypt at the hand of God. So it is that whoever celebrates the Passover meal participates in the event and shares its effects. It is a *remembrance* of this act of salvation. The Greek word for remembrance is **anamnesis**, the same word New Testament writers use for what Jesus said at the Last Supper: 'Do this *in remembrance* of me.' Our remembrance of what the Lord himself did and commanded at the Last Supper is our remembrance of his sacrifice on the cross, proclaimed anew each time we break the bread he gives. Through sharing 'the bread that we break' and 'the cup of blessing that we bless' (using St Paul's words in 1 Corinthians 10.16), we are united as one believing people with Jesus – body, soul and divinity – who has died, has risen and will come again.

St Paul, witnessing to the words of Jesus at the Last Supper, also gives us his understanding of the Eucharist in the passage which follows his account of what Jesus said and did then: 'as often as you eat this bread and drink the cup, you proclaim the Lord's death until he comes' (1 Corinthians 11.26). We remember in order to share/proclaim with others the saving events of Calvary. But not only that, we do it in order to be united with Christ in his sacrificial work:

> The cup of blessing that we bless, is it not a participation in the blood of Christ? The bread that we break, is it not a participation in the body of Christ? Because there is one bread, we who are many are one body, for we all partake of the one bread.
> (1 Corinthians 10.16–17)

The Eucharist as the enduring sign of Jesus

The bread on which the Christian feeds in the Eucharist is Jesus himself. St John sets out this teaching from Jesus in chapter 6 of his Gospel. This is his commentary on the miracle of the Feeding of the Five Thousand, which happens, significantly, at the time of Passover, the Jewish feast which recalls God leading his captive people out of slavery in Egypt. On that exhausting journey, the people ate manna, bread provided by God as food to sustain them. Now, in this miraculous event, Jesus feeds a large number of people who had followed him 'because they saw the signs that he was doing' (6.2). **Signs** is St John's preferred word for Jesus' miracles because they are pointers to his divine nature and his glory. Then next day Jesus gives his teaching about the bread over which 'he had given thanks' (6.11). With the Passover traditions in mind, Jesus says to those who question him,

> 'Truly, truly, I say to you, it was not Moses who gave you the bread from heaven, but my Father gives you the true bread from heaven. For the bread of God is he who comes down from heaven and gives life to the world.' (John 6.32–33)

Their answer is, 'Sir, give us this bread always' (6.34), echoing the Church's prayer, 'Give us this day our daily bread.'

Jesus continues, saying: 'I am the bread of life; whoever comes to me shall not hunger, and whoever believes in me shall never thirst' (6.35). When this incredible statement is disputed, Jesus expands on his claim to be the bread of life:

> 'Your fathers ate the manna in the wilderness, and they died. This is the bread that comes down from heaven, so that one may eat of it and not die. I am the living bread that came down from heaven. If anyone eats of this bread, he will live for ever. And the bread that I will give for the life of the world is my flesh.'
> (John 6.49–51)

This talk of eating his flesh causes more dispute, but he goes still further:

> 'Truly, truly, I say to you, unless you eat the flesh of the Son of Man and drink his blood, you have no life in you. Whoever feeds on my flesh and drinks my blood has eternal life, and I will raise him up on the last day. For my flesh is true food, and my blood is true drink. Whoever feeds on my flesh and drinks my blood abides in me, and I in him. As the living Father sent me, and I live because of the Father, so whoever feeds on me, he also will live because of me. This is the bread that came down from heaven, not like the bread the fathers ate and died. Whoever feeds on this bread will live for ever.'
> (John 6.53–58)

Why bread?

Bread is a symbol of life, but it is also a basic source of sustenance for all people, rich and poor alike. And our ordinary lives can be transformed by the extraordinary life of Jesus, our bread being made into something totally life-giving and life-enhancing. Jesus came, says St John, that we might 'have life and have it abundantly' (10.10). No wonder, then, that Jesus says to the disciples, 'I am the living bread that came down from heaven. If anyone eats of this bread, he will live for ever. And the bread that I will give for the life of the world is my flesh' (6.51). Here we should remember that St John is the Evangelist who describes the birth of Jesus, this gift of living bread come down from heaven, as **Incarnation**: 'the Word became flesh and dwelt among us, and we have seen his glory, glory as of the only Son from the Father, full of grace and truth' (1.14). And 'from his fullness have we all received' (1.16). God's loving gift of his incarnate Son is abundantly generous: 'I am the bread of life; whoever comes to me shall not hunger' (6.35). The part bread plays in the drama of our salvation is no accident: it takes us to the heart of why God is our Father who always wants the best for us, who wishes to provide for us food that is life-giving, and who asks us to pray to him as Jesus taught, 'Give us this day our daily bread.'

Jesus is known to us in the breaking of the bread

St John tells us that the other disciples reported to Thomas, who had not been with them on the Easter evening when the risen Jesus appeared, 'We have seen the Lord' (20.25). St Luke's unique addition to the account of that day is his story of two disciples who, that evening, met a traveller on the road to Emmaus. It was Jesus, but 'their eyes were kept from recognizing him' (24.16). To confront their sadness and disappointment at the death of the one in whom they had hoped, as well as their confusion at the report of his empty tomb, Jesus reminds them of what the Scriptures said concerning these things. Though still unrecognized, Jesus is invited to supper at their journey's end where, at table, he takes bread, blesses it, breaks it and gives it to them. St Luke then says, 'Their eyes were opened, and they recognized him' (24.31). Straightaway returning to Jerusalem, they found the Eleven and others gathered together, who reported to them that 'the Lord has risen indeed' (24.34). These two disciples add their story of what happened to them in words which, for the Church down the ages, have given form and substance to its belief about the presence of Jesus in the Eucharist, 'he was known to them in the breaking of the bread' (24.35). As the Last Supper in the upper room prepared the disciples for the events of Good Friday, so the supper at Emmaus presents to us the Eucharist as the means by which we know and recognize the risen Lord and experience his presence in our lives. At the Eucharist we meet Jesus whose promise to his disciples was 'I will not leave you as orphans; I will come to you' (John 14.18). We truly meet him who was made flesh, who died and was raised by the power of the Father. We meet him as did those two disciples on the road to Emmaus and, having met him in Holy Communion, we can say, like them, 'Did not our hearts burn within us?' (Luke 24.32). And, like all the Apostles, we can declare joyfully and as a proclamation of faith, 'We have seen the Lord' (cf. John 20.25).

Some questions to consider

Can you think of a time when the Eucharist has spoken to you/touched you personally?

_____

_____

_____

_____

'The Eucharist is a fire which inflames us' (St John Chrysostom). Do you feel this is a helpful idea?

_____

_____

_____

_____

Do you think the presence of Jesus in the Eucharist may be different from his presence elsewhere?

_____

_____

_____

_____

_____

In conclusion

▶ Watch the **video** at <www.breadoflifecourse.co.uk /eucharist>

The video is a montage of the Eucharist in multiple contexts, set to a beautiful recording of the song *Bread of Life*, by Joanne Boyce and Mike Stanley. The emphasis here is on the *importance* of the Eucharist in the Church today and its role in Christian unity.

 End with the **liturgy** on p. 2 or p. 3

After the module

What have you learned from this week's module?

_____

_____

_____

_____

_____

We would love to hear your feedback on *Bread of Life* at <www.surveymonkey.com/BreadofLife>. Your feedback will help us to develop the course further and is really important to us.

MODULE 2

2

He has reconciled us to God

Aim of this module

This module looks at what it means to be reconciled to God, and why we participate in repentance and absolution as preparation for receiving the Eucharist.

Way into this module

 Begin with the **liturgy** on p. 1

Watch the **video** at <www.breadoflifecourse.co.uk /prodigal-son>

The video shows the story of the Prodigal Son, filmed in a contemporary urban setting. The biblical text is printed at the beginning of the Main talk, below.

Main talk

((●)) Also available as a **podcast** at <www.breadoflifecourse .co.uk/maintalk2>

The Parable of the Prodigal Son
And he said, 'There was a man who had two sons. And the younger of them said to his father, "Father, give me the share of property that is coming to me." And he divided his property between them. Not many days later, the younger son gathered all he had and took a journey into a far country, and there he squandered his property in reckless living. And when he had spent

everything, a severe famine arose in that country, and he began to be in need. So, he went and hired himself out to one of the citizens of that country, who sent him into his fields to feed pigs. And he was longing to be fed with the pods that the pigs ate, and no one gave him anything.

'But when he came to himself, he said, "How many of my father's hired servants have more than enough bread, but I perish here with hunger! I will arise and go to my father, and I will say to him, 'Father, I have sinned against heaven and before you. I am no longer worthy to be called your son. Treat me as one of your hired servants.'" And he arose and came to his father. But while he was still a long way off, his father saw him and felt compassion, and ran and embraced him and kissed him. And the son said to him, "Father, I have sinned against heaven and before you. I am no longer worthy to be called your son." But the father said to his servants, "Bring quickly the best robe, and put it on him, and put a ring on his hand, and shoes on his feet. And bring the fattened calf and kill it, and let us eat and celebrate. For this my son was dead, and is alive again; he was lost, and is found." And they began to celebrate.

'Now his older son was in the field, and as he came and drew near to the house, he heard music and dancing. And he called one of the servants and asked what these things meant. And he said to him, "Your brother has come, and your father has killed the fattened calf, because he has received him back safe and sound." But he was angry and refused to go in. His

father came out and entreated him, but he answered his father, "Look, these many years I have served you, and I never disobeyed your command, yet you never gave me a young goat, that I might celebrate with my friends. But when this son of yours came, who has devoured your property with prostitutes, you killed the fattened calf for him!" And he said to him, "Son, you are always with me, and all that is mine is yours. It was fitting to celebrate and be glad, for this your brother was dead, and is alive; he was lost, and is found."'
(Luke 15.11–32)

Going home

Perhaps on holiday overseas you realize you don't know how to get back to your hotel. If you could speak the language, you could ask the way! Or maybe out in the car your satnav gives up the ghost! Panic sets in, the blood pressure rises and from deep within a voice cries 'Where am I?'

The parable of the Prodigal Son is about someone who is lost and finds himself asking that very question. It's a striking phrase Luke uses when the son is at his lowest point amongst the pigs – 'he came to himself' (15.17). The original language of the text literally means 'he entered into himself'. The prodigal son looks into his heart, into the depths of himself, to the attitudes, desires and emotions that influence our behaviour. He realizes he's adrift. He has lost sight of what's true and important. He grasps the fact that he needs to reorientate himself and return home.

What is Jesus saying to us here? Basically, how easy it is to follow the wrong course, and how important it is to 'enter into ourselves' and recognize those desires/emotions that motivate us.

We don't know what prompted the prodigal son to leave home. Maybe he was simply bored with life, and began to drift into unhealthy ways of finding self-worth. It happens. He wanted a quick fix and imagined he'd find fulfilment in money, lifestyle and gratification – things the day-to-day routine with his father and kin, the sheer 'ordinariness' of life, just didn't give. He wanted something better than the existence he knew, but lost all sense of who he really was in the process.

OK, we may not be going off the rails quite as dramatically as that. But we can feel restless about the 'place we find ourselves in' and begin looking for something better. One syndrome around presently is FOMO, Fear of Missing Out: we imagine, occasionally at least, that other people are having a better time than we are, and long for more instant gratification than the immediate routines of life are giving.

St Augustine (AD 354–430), one of the greatest Christian thinkers, addresses this dilemma in his autobiography *The Confessions*. As a young man he felt that God was distant from him, but realizes eventually that, rather than the problem being the absence of God, it was *he himself* who wasn't there. Too occupied with short-term satisfaction, he hadn't entered deeply enough into himself to discover God waiting patiently for him there in the depths of his own soul.

Called by love

The prodigal son realises he's lost and comes to his senses. Within his heart he discovers a compass pointing him back to his father. The story continues with Jesus movingly describing the open arms of a father who runs to meet a wayward child. Those who return home to God are always met with mercy.

Every Eucharist begins with the recognition that we carry within us a tangle of thoughts and feelings. Sometimes we arrive with a sense of being lost, of not being 'in a good place', conscious that things aren't how they ought to be in our relationship with God and others. So before we move on to anything else, we pause in the Penitential Rite to 'enter into ourselves' and find our way home to the freedom of God's children.

In the well-known poem 'Love', George Herbert reflects on the process of penitentially acknowledging before God that we are sinners, in order that we may hear more clearly the welcome God gives. The soul draws back from God 'guilty of dust and sin', yet the insistent mercy of the loving Father seeks out the wayward to bring them home:

> Love took my hand and smiling did reply,
>   'Who made the eyes but I?'
> 'Truth, Lord; but I have marr'd them: let my shame
>   Go where it doth deserve.'
> 'And know you not,' says Love, 'Who bore the blame?'
>   'My dear, then I will serve.'
> 'You must sit down,' says Love, 'and taste my meat.'
>   So I did sit and eat.

Feeling repentant, realizing things are not as they should be, that's a sign that God's grace is at work in our lives. We've become attentive to the voice of Love drawing us home. This great truth runs profoundly counter to the culture of our age, where the failings of those in the public eye are often seized upon by the media, where guilt and blame are the name of the game. The pattern of each and every Eucharist tells us that, yes, our sins *do* matter, that not everything can be glossed over, but that even our worst failures don't mean God closes the door on us. Mass begins by seeking and offering forgiveness, by putting relationships right – with God and one another.

One of the surprise box-office hits of the 1990s was *Dead Man Walking*, based on the true story of Sister Helen Prejean, a prison visitor who meets rapist and murderer Matthew Poncelet and accompanies him on death row. A harrowing story, it doesn't try to score points for or against the death penalty. We see something of the brutality of Matthew's crime and its effects on the families of his victims. We also see Matthew's own family background and the way he comes to face his death. But what's most striking is how Sister Helen gets Matthew to own up, rather than blame his parents or even his victims. Her painstaking work allows Matthew to admit what he has done and finally have the dignity of both claiming his deeds as his own and being able to ask for forgiveness.

The prodigal son regains his dignity when he comes to his senses and returns home to ask his father's mercy. We too are given the dignity to admit what we've done and say we're sorry as every Eucharist begins. Posture is important in liturgy – it matters whether we stand, sit or kneel. Interestingly, for the Penitential Rite in the newer forms of the Eucharist, like those in *Common Worship* or the Roman Rite, we are standing. It is appropriate, in terms of human dignity, that we stand upright (we evolved from *homo erectus*) when we own up and ask for forgiveness, because receiving God's mercy sets us on our feet as his children.

Many Christians regard the Sacrament of Reconciliation (Confession and Absolution) as an important part of their spiritual discipline, a more personal and rigorous way of admitting sin and knowing forgiveness than is possible in the short rite at the start of the Eucharist. This sacrament directly addresses the tendency in all of us to think we are not worthy of forgiveness. It's hard to forgive ourselves for past faults. Repentance and reconciliation assure us, however, that we *are* forgiven, and can feel the grasp of a loving Father's hand, who leads us to his banquet of life and love.

The Penitential Rite at Mass celebrates our human worth and dignity. Being welcomed home and assured of the Father's loving attention should make all the difference to the way we see ourselves and others. We stand shoulder to shoulder with one another, equal recipients of God's mercy and grace. Knowing that power of forgiveness in our own lives, we are given confidence to display it in our relationships with others too.

The God who sets a feast

In Jesus' parable we are not given the father's words to his wayward child upon his return, he simply relates what the father does – he runs and embraces and kisses him, and instructs his servants to prepare a banquet. The banquet is the father's gift to his son to show that he has been forgiven. Similarly, in the Eucharist we 'come to' and return to the Father to ask for mercy, as guests at the banquet set for us. We are welcome.

In the Penitential Rite we not only look 'into ourselves', but also outwards to the neighbours we stand alongside. The Prayers of Penitence belong to the start of the Eucharist because they are not just about us, but also about how we wound other people – not least by how we so easily become alienated from the very family with whom we gather.

We can't overlook the character of the elder brother in the parable of the Prodigal Son. In his resentment at the welcome the prodigal is receiving, he holds back from the feast and refuses to be drawn into the celebration. Acknowledging that we are all equal recipients of the mercy of God, that we all stand under the cross (of which the Eucharist is the sacrament), means that we must let go of any chip on our shoulder or resentment we harbour.

If you stop to think about it, what we do whenever we gather together to celebrate the Eucharist is something profoundly counter-cultural. We live in a society that tries to compartmentalize people: we are either young or old; single or have a partner; we have different likes, aspirations and interests. Perhaps in our own country, we are aware of that divide more than ever at the moment in terms of political debate. But when we are at Mass, we come together from across all divides to proclaim that we belong to God and to one another. In the *Common Worship* Rite for the Eucharist, we hear these words: 'Christ is our peace; he has reconciled us to God in one body by the cross. We meet in his name and share his peace.'

We 'enter into ourselves' to discover our need for God's mercy, but we also take a look around us at the new family that is being formed at the altar and gathered into the grace, mercy and peace of God.

Some questions to consider

Can you think of an occasion when you've been lost physically? What did that feel like? Has there been a time in your life when you've felt lost spiritually? What did that feel like?

_____

_____

_____

_____

_____

Can you think of a situation globally or nationally where someone admitting they were wrong and saying sorry has changed things? Does our attendance at the Eucharist make us more forgiving people?

Does coming to the Eucharist feel like coming home? If so, how?

In conclusion

▶ Watch the **video** at <www.breadoflifecourse.co.uk/truth>

The video is called *Absolute Truth: A restorative justice story*. It follows the journey of a husband and wife, Ray and Vi Donovan, whose son is brutally murdered by a gang of youths. After a period of grief that almost rips the family apart, the couple embark on a journey of reflection and self-discovery, which ultimately leads them to find it within themselves to meet and forgive the perpetrators of the crime.

((♀)) Listen to the **podcast** at <www.breadoflifecourse.co.uk /sarah-gillard-faulkner>

In this podcast, Sarah Gillard-Faulkner offers brief reflections on the *Absolute Truth* video. You will also find some relevant resource material on p. 127.

Listen to the **podcast** at <www.breadoflifecourse.co.uk/joan-whyman>

In this podcast, Joan Whyman talks about discovering the Sacrament of Reconciliation.

In conclusion

End with the **liturgy** on p. 2 or p. 3

After the module

What did you learn from this week's module?

_____

_____

_____

_____

_____

We would love to hear your feedback on *Bread of Life* at <www.surveymonkey.com/BreadofLife>. Your feedback will help us to develop the course further and is really important to us.

MODULE 3

3

The word of the Lord

Aim of this module

This module examines the importance of Scripture, giving an overview of the arc of Scripture, and looking in detail at the biblical passages that inform our understanding of the Eucharist.

Way into this module

 Begin with the **liturgy** on p. 1

▶ Watch the **video** at <www.breadoflifecourse.co.uk/road-to-emmaus>

The video shows the Road to Emmaus story, filmed in a contemporary setting.

Main talk

((○)) Also available as a **podcast** at <www.breadoflifecourse.co.uk/maintalk3>

Looking for Jesus

Who is Jesus? You might have preferred a single written biography. Instead, you have been led to a chest full of material and invited to search through the evidence that lies within, to discover for yourself who Jesus is. It's more work, of course, but that work will be rewarded by a truly personal encounter with the Son of God.

You will read letters from his friends; you will share the struggles of a people who tried to make real, even before

Jesus was born, the power of his sacrificial death by their temple sacrifices; you will be puzzled by the fitful history of those who tried to express his teaching; you will read pages you do not understand; but nonetheless in the Scriptures you will meet the living God face to face, and hear his authentic voice.

The Lord Jesus Christ, our Saviour, the Word of God, has been revealed, by the power of the Holy Spirit, through the words of the Scriptures. This is what we believe, and what, through experience, we have come to know.

The power of these words

How can so extraordinary a claim be true? Because God *wishes* to reveal himself to us, and because this encounter with his Son is about **meaning**. We listen to these words not to discover what the world is, but what the world means.

Don't, therefore, spend your time trying to work out how this can be. Don't find excuses to put off the work: get down to it, read the words or hear them read. Search the Scriptures, as generations of Jews and Christians have done, and you will find the Lord.

If God simply wanted us to be better people, would he not have given us a shorter, simpler text – a how-to-be-a-good-person manual – and left it at that? No, God wants more, which is why he offers the possibility of getting to know his Son, to develop a deep and lasting relationship with him, which will take both time and commitment.

Working with what God has given us

The Scriptures are not given to us for our entertainment, but so that we might discover the Lord Jesus and hear his voice. This givenness of the Scriptures can be a source of assurance to us: any time we come across a difficulty or challenge, or are intimidated by the lists of names and numbers, or begin to wonder at this man who curses fig trees, we can remind ourselves that it's the same for every Christian, of whatever nation or century.

The Bible is always a gift, not an imposition: this is the way to Christ.

Start with the New Testament. The four Gospels most clearly show us our Lord, in his life and death. We are all familiar with at least some parts of those four accounts. In other books of the New Testament, mostly in the letters from the Apostles, we are introduced to larger, more abstract ideas of sin and grace, hope and salvation. Grappling with these will enlarge our understanding of who it is we seek and what he has done for us, and help us to reflect on how we can respond more fully in our lives.

Why the Old Testament?

Why should we read the Old Testament, which is more distant and more indirect in its revelation? The answer is because many of the most important themes in the New Testament are foreshadowed in the Old. We can never fully understand what is going on in the events of the New Testament unless we have some idea of their Old Testament context.

In first-century Palestine, to talk of God was, by definition, to talk of the One God: nine hundred years before, Elijah had to fight on Mount Carmel for the truth that there is only one God (1 Kings 18). In his day, you might say, this was the gospel message – the good news in the face of the polytheism of the pagans.

Christians know that Jesus has atoned for our sins: Isaiah could only reach for this vision in his beautiful poem of the Suffering Servant. The book of Job wrestles with the problem of suffering with no knowledge of a Saviour, and is all the more powerful for that.

Consider also the Psalms. Some will be familiar, some less so, and many verses are difficult and disturbing to read. The Psalms tell us of the sorrows and the joys which our ancestors in the faith have shared with God – people who communed with him without the full support of the Church and the sacraments which we now enjoy.

What sort of books are the Scriptures?

Chapter 5 of the book of Judges, the Song of Deborah, may well be the oldest text in the Bible that has come down to us, virtually unchanged and unedited from more than 3,200 years ago. Set in the dark centuries when the tribes of Israel were locked in a life-and-death struggle for their survival, it celebrates the way in which they were led to glorious victory by this enigmatic woman.

The Lord's promise was the bedrock of the tribes' identity. His law was their constitution. In a world without police or social services or hospitals or universities or local councils, it was their entire social framework. From this, they developed their song (as above) and their literature.

In Solomon's court, in the Jerusalem of the ninth century BC, a formal bureaucracy grew up to administer his kingdom. Those involved needed to learn writing skills, and one of the texts for students to copy would have been Proverbs chapter 10 (or something like it). This was the beginning of wisdom literature – a study of the world in order to understand it according to the working of God's law.

A growing richness

Mix song and wisdom and fast-forward a few centuries, and we come to the teaching of the Prophets. This teaching deepened its recipients' moral and social awareness, so that, when invasion, defeat and destruction came at the hands of Babylon (twice in 598 and 587 BC), they possessed a rich literary and theological framework. This enabled them to survive as a people, who trusted that, through repentance and obedience, their relationship with God would be repaired.

The slow restoration of Judah (itself the remnant of Israel) under the Persians, the rebuilding of Jerusalem and the new political realities of the age of empire (the Persians were replaced by the Greeks who were superseded by the Romans) all led to still greater sophistication in the writing, wisdom and theology of the people of God.

From these later writings, there grew a theology of hope, a turning to the future and a deepening of spiritual perception that provided the context for the coming of the Christ.

The Prayer Book's famous collect

The Scriptures are not as simple as a novel, as the above historical sketch indicates, so nor can be our reading of them. It may seem rather old-fashioned, but the Book of Common Prayer's well-known Collect for Bible Sunday offers both a valuable prayer (to use before or after reading) and a helpful prompt:

> Blessed Lord, who hast caused all holy Scriptures to be written for our learning: Grant that we may in such wise hear them, read, mark, learn, and inwardly digest them, that by patience and comfort of thy holy Word, we may embrace and ever hold fast the blessed hope of everlasting life, which thou hast given us in our Saviour Jesus Christ.

Consider then its five reminders.

Hear A first encounter with the Bible may be in a church service; we hear it with others; it is a shared experience.

Read If we wish to go further and deeper, there must be an individual and personal involvement; by reading, we draw the words into our self.

Mark We need to pay attention; the words are to flow into us, not over us. In so doing we begin to draw our own markers on the text, to place our own framework on this vast collection of writings. This is important for we are not merely passive.

Learn With time we will become familiar with the stories, the people, the triumphs and disasters, the advice and the warnings. Then, as we listen to one narrative, we will be able to remember others and add further meaning to what's in front of us.

Inwardly digest Jesus himself cited Scripture (Deuteronomy 8.3) to make the point, 'Man shall not live by bread alone, but by every word that comes from the mouth of God' (Matthew 4.4, ESV). This is, literally, our spiritual food.

The Word here on earth

We speak of the challenge of reading the Scriptures. What many find difficult to grasp is how the perfect Word of God is found in the ordinary words of the Bible. How can the Scriptures be both divine and human? In a sentence: if Jesus is both fully divine and fully human, then so too are the Scriptures that reveal him. It is no mistake that they are inspired by God and written by humans – God has deliberately used the imperfections of the biblical writers to reveal his Son. The Word is not in heaven, as Moses assured us, it 'is very near to you; it is in your mouth and in your heart' (Deuteronomy 30.14, NRSV). The words are so close to us because they are human as well as divine, just like Christ himself.

The words of the Bible invite us into something beyond what we see written on the page, precisely so that we do not stop there, but encounter the person of Jesus Christ who is behind these texts. 'The word of the Lord endures for ever,' says St Peter (1 Peter 1.25, NIV), but how it is received and acted upon changes with each one of us.

The value of familiarity

We should read and reread the Scriptures as familiarity helps us to engage more deeply with their words and take them to heart. A childhood memory of the parable of the Sower is not enough: each of us must hear or read it again, not because we have forgotten the story, but because each phrase and word is important if we are to grasp its meaning properly.

In our lifelong relationship with God, we need to listen to the words he has given us. When we speak of them as 'living' words, we mean that each time we hear them they are newly spoken. A simple analogy would be when your spouse says, 'I love you.' The meaning is both familiar and new.

The power of the words

So the words of Scripture are not only informative, giving us information, but also performative, meaning they can do things. To take the clearest example: the Lord's Prayer is not telling us *about* prayer; it *is* prayer.

Consider Jesus, when tempted by the devil in the wilderness. His threefold reply, 'It is written', followed by a quotation from the Scriptures, is categorical and definitive (Matthew 4.4, 7, 10, ESV). He's not offering the opening opinions in a discussion! In each case, Jesus' words defeat the devil's temptation.

As the centurion, whose servant was lying ill at home, understood, the Lord's word alone can heal (Matthew 8.13). In a wider sense, all the words in Scripture have power through him. As noted in the Bible study, the words of the two disciples to Jesus at Emmaus, 'Stay with us' (Luke 24.29), can be for us a prayer of real power precisely because of the context in which they were first used.

The words of eternal life

As we'll also learn from the Bible study, Jesus himself told his disciples that the (Hebrew) Scriptures spoke about him. It was with this understanding that the four Gospels were recorded. As John himself explains, 'these [the words of his Gospel] are written so that you may believe that Jesus is the Christ, the Son of God, and that believing you may have life in his name' (20.31, ESV).

Some questions to consider

What do you hope to receive from reading the Scriptures?

_____

_____

_____

_____

_____

What passage of the Bible have you found most helpful or most difficult?

The word of the Lord

_____

_____

_____

_____

_____

How do you understand the power of the words of the Bible?

_____

_____

_____

_____

Where is Jesus?

An Old Testament example. Take these two powerful, imaginative word pictures, two connected dramas of almost gothic exaggeration, and ask the simple question, 'Where was Jesus in all this?' Read chapters 3 and 7 of the book of Daniel. Written as a response to intense persecution, they give a vision of the truth behind the truth.

The theme of creation

A single uniting theme for the whole of the Bible? A good candidate must surely be creation, from God the Creator. Is creation only in the past, the Garden of Eden of Genesis 1 and 2? What about, say Psalm 102.18 (ESV), that tells us that God continues to create:

> Let this be recorded for a generation to come,
>> so that a people yet to be created may praise the LORD:

or the New Jerusalem of Revelation 21 and 22 which seems a promise for the future?

Consider the questions

One of the simplest ways to hear for yourself the voice of Jesus in the Gospels is, carefully and deliberately, to consider the questions – those Jesus asks of those around him, and the questions that are asked of him. Imagine yourself to be there; reflect on what the question might mean, and think about the answer you would give to or expect from our Lord.

The challenging bits?

The book of Leviticus is often a part of the Old Testament that people find difficult and challenging. This can be the book that those who set out to read the whole Bible from beginning to end traditionally give up on. It sums up everything we dislike most. Read chapters 16 to 19, slowly, sincerely and with humility, realizing that you might find it uncomfortable because of the way it contrasts human sinfulness with God's absolute holiness. You still may not like Leviticus, but show respect, for it was from this context we were first taught, 'Love your neighbour as yourself' (Leviticus 19.18, ESV).

Reading the whole Bible

Rule 1: don't begin with Genesis. Rule 2: spend twice as much time reading the New Testament as the Old. Make a list and tick the books off. Move around. If you have never read the Bible before, begin like this: 1 John, Ruth, Mark, Amos, Galatians. Got started? Brilliant. Now talk with your parish priest or share with others, and keep reading. Isaiah 40–55, Luke, Genesis . . .

Reading the Lectionary

If the previous panel about reading the whole Bible is too daunting, consider reading the Lectionary, and in doing so sharing the work of the Church. Find an online Lectionary; search 'Mass readings' or ask a member of the clergy. Read the texts beforehand, so that when you hear them they will carry more meaning. As you develop the discipline, you might read more around the actual reading, to put it in its context.

> **The Bible in church**
> There is a constant temptation in prayer and worship to focus on ourselves and our needs. The Scriptures act like an oasis in the wilderness – however far we wander, we are drawn back to the water of life. With the Bible, by the power of the Holy Spirit, as the source of our prayer and worship, we are not only sustained but kept close to the Lord.

(((◦))) Listen to the **podcast** at <www.breadoflifecourse.co.uk /scriptureoverview>

The podcast gives an overview of Scripture and the script is printed below.

What is Scripture?

The phrase I especially like is the one popular with Evangelicals, 'the Word of God written', as opposed to 'the words of God written'.

When we speak of 'the Word of God' we mean the Lord Jesus Christ, Son of God, *the* Word of God. Received, not here in bread and wine, but through the words of the books of the Bible.

So, really, it's not 'Scripture and the words of God' but the other way around, 'the Word of God and the Scriptures'?

Exactly. The Word is singular, and the books of the Bible are many, but all speak of Jesus, the Word made flesh.

Can you give a picture for this idea?
Think of the climax of the first part of the Eucharist. The deacon stands in the midst of the people; everyone, people and clergy alike, turns towards the Gospel book; the gospel is read. The Word of God – Jesus – is made present through the words written, spoken for all to share.

Are you saying it's the same sort of presence?
In the sacrament, Christ comes to us directly in the elements of bread and wine. In the Scriptures, the words are mediated through our mind and feelings, and interpreted through the teaching of the Church. The process may be more complex and less direct, but the words will teach, inform, enthuse and inspire us.

So are we a People of the Book?
Actually, no. We are a People of the Word, the Lord Jesus himself; and we learn about him mostly through the various books of the Bible which the Holy Spirit has inspired the authors to write.

And how were the books of the Bible put together?
The Bible is made up of the Old and the New Testaments. Both are the collection of books which the rabbis of Israel (in the case of the Old Testament), and the early Church Fathers (in the case of the New), regarded as genuinely inspired by God. Age, history of use, and the claim of authorship were among the criteria for making these decisions. It has always been an important principle that this must be a collective decision of the whole Church, since the Holy Spirit works

primarily through the body of Christ as a whole, rather than individuals who claim to have had private revelations.

Back to the serious stuff. What are the books of the Bible?
We start with four Gospels, each in a different way drawing us into the life and death of Jesus. Then various letters, from Paul and other Apostles, sent to the early church communities, by way of encouragement, instruction, answering questions or settling arguments. There's an account of the growth of the early Church, called Acts; and the book of Revelation – a vision of the heavenly kingdom, giving encouragement to those suffering persecution.

That's the New Testament. Why four Gospels, and not just one?
The Gospels are not only biographies, recording the events of Christ's life. They were written to draw us into that life, to enable us to gain a relationship with him. If we only had one Gospel we would have a rather 2D account of Jesus. The fact that we have four – each with its own unique elements – means that we are asked to work with the texts, view the key events from different angles, and so come to a deeper and fuller understanding of who Jesus is.

If Matthew emphasises the Jewish context, and Luke the universal setting of Jesus' teaching, if Mark is vivid and immediate, and John deeply reflective, then it is clear we have been given much richer perspectives than any one Evangelist could achieve individually.

And the Old Testament?

The most ancient part, the five books of Moses, gives us a theological account of creation, God's relationship with mankind, and how that relationship was broken because of sin. As the story progresses, we see how human beings' attempts to restore that relationship end in failure, but that God has his own plan for reconciliation, which he promises will be fulfilled. In the history of Israel, we see a prototype of how that plan will one day come about, and we are reminded of the need to remain faithful. The prophets of Israel warn against sin and idolatry, but also offer encouragement that salvation will come to God's people, even when their prospects look bleak. We also have a collection of writings such as Job, the Psalms, Proverbs, the beautiful love poem the Song of Songs, and the austere meditation of Ecclesiastes, which help us to grow in wisdom, maturity and love of God, especially in the face of suffering.

Are some parts of the Bible more useful than others?

Certain books of the Bible can leave us wondering how useful they really are. Think of the book of Numbers with its great lists of figures, or the detailed measurements for the Temple building in 2 Chronicles. Yet even where we may initially struggle to see the usefulness of certain texts, Jesus is always just beneath the surface. For example, in the descriptions of the Temple building we learn that it is God who decides how he may be approached, on what terms, with what offerings and by whom – which points us towards Jesus, who offers the perfect sacrifice that allows all who believe in him to approach God freely.

Wouldn't it have been better if it had all been written at one time?

It might have been easier to read, but it would not, absolutely not, have been better. Think of it like this: if life were simple we wouldn't need the Scriptures; we could sort it all out just by being good to others. The books of the Bible were written in response to real crises: persecution, slavery, war, famine, exile, inter-family quarrels and injustice – all the result of our alienation from God because of sin. It is a record of how we have tried and failed to get back to God on our own terms, and God's gracious love in bringing us back on his terms.

You're saying the Bible is not an easy read?

The Bible *is* demanding. But don't worry: it is hugely rewarding. Don't sit down and think you can just read it, like a novel or an instruction manual. Approach it with respect. Offer a prayer beforehand, for help and guidance; accept that this is not the sort of text you would choose, but that it allows you, slowly but surely, to speak with God; read it bit by bit, and remember that God is speaking to you, even if you do not yet understand; be assured, from the whole history of the Church, that such time of regular, careful reading of the Scriptures is never lost.

Should all Christians read the Bible regularly?

Yes. Christ comes to you, fully and completely, in the sacrament of his body and blood, but the Bible helps us to know him more intimately. The Scriptures are a gift. They draw us closer to the Lord and, in doing so, draw us closer

to ourselves, and to the mystery of our life and salvation in
Christ.

**It goes like this: We could just receive passively, but God
is offering us the opportunity to be involved, to be drawn
into his work of salvation, to see ourselves and the world
more clearly?**
Absolutely. The Scriptures are an invitation; something we
can use and share throughout our faith journey. As St Paul
said, 'All Scripture is breathed out by God and profitable
for teaching, for reproof, for correction, and for training in
righteousness' (2 Timothy 3.16, ESV).

Which brings us to the Lectionary.
For every Sunday Eucharist throughout the year, the
Church has chosen three readings; these are taken from
the Old Testament, followed by a psalm that is said
or sung, from the New Testament epistles and from
the Gospels. This achieves two things: we hear a good
selection of the most important and valuable texts from
the Bible; and we hear them together. Whatever we might
think of the choices made, these are the official texts, and
we hear them with the whole Church throughout the
world.

Why is this so important?
It's the clearest expression, I think, that the Scriptures are
a gift from God. They are part of the givenness of our faith,
and we hear them as a universal, worldwide family.

Can you go into that a bit more?

Our faith is not about 'general truths'. It is focused specifically on one man, at one place and at one time, who claimed to be God. Yet everyone, in every age and on every continent, can meet him in these pages, here and now.

We say, rightly, that the Eucharist is the Sacrament of Unity. But it is important to realize that much of this unity is achieved by our reading and knowledge of the Scriptures. These readings are our shared heritage: our regular reflection upon them draws us back to God and to one another.

OK, give an example.

The book of Deuteronomy is a passionate sermon exhorting people to a deeper understanding of God's law. We can imagine ourselves in the hot, dusty plain of Moab, more than three thousand years ago, listening to Moses speak, 'I have set before you life and death, blessings and curses. Now choose life, so that you and your children may live' (Deuteronomy 30.19, NIV). And we can hear it again, now, where we are, knowing, as we do, that the Lord Jesus is our life and our law.

You obviously love that passage. Do you have others?

What about Peter's first letter? When one knows that it was written to young people, quite poor, many of them slaves, living under the threat of persecution, on the edge of the Roman Empire, in a culture of fear, the Apostle's words are full of warmth and generosity, power and encouragement.

I happen to think the book of Jonah is one of the master-pieces of world literature, an exquisite story underlining the great problem of love, the interplay between justice and mercy, between punishment and compassion. Both engaging and deeply moving.

And the hard passages?
Perhaps you're thinking of the Old Testament? Amos, from the eighth century BC, is sometimes called the prophet of doom: 'Prepare to meet thy God' (Amos 4.12, KJV). Yet it is from him that we learn it is far better to be condemned by the living God than to be blessed by a false god. The Lord's Old Testament denunciation is the first step to the gospel of salvation. God's condemnation is a grace, truly!

And the bits in between?
As I said before, the Scriptures are a gold mine of riches. It is for us to hunt around and find the treasure for ourselves. On the surface some may seem irrelevant. In 2 Timothy 4.13 (ESV) Paul wrote, 'When you come, bring the cloak that I left with Carpus at Troas', as trivial a verse as one could imagine; and yet whole sermons have been written, of real worth, on these few words.

You mean, really, that they are more than just words?
Yes. In the end, they come from God, and draw us back to God. They are our spiritual food. As Jeremiah put it, evoking the Eucharist itself, 'Your words were found, and I ate them, and your words became to me a joy and the

delight of my heart, for I am called by your name, O LORD, God of hosts' (Jeremiah 15.16).

That is why all of us in the Church must encourage ourselves, and our brothers and sisters, to read the Bible. Not just to read about it, or what other people say about it, but to read the very words given to us. They are our life; they are the word of the Lord.

((○)) Listen to the **podcast** at <www.breadoflifecourse.co.uk /road-to-emmaus-study>

This is a recording of the Road to Emmaus passage, printed below. The passage is followed by a blank page on which you may like to make notes. Your leader may ask you questions.

On the Road to Emmaus

That very day two of them were going to a village named Emmaus, about seven miles from Jerusalem, and they were talking with each other about all these things that had happened. While they were talking and discussing together, Jesus himself drew near and went with them. But their eyes were kept from recognizing him. And he said to them, 'What is this conversation that you are holding with each other as you walk?' And they stood still, looking sad. Then one of them, named Cleopas, answered him, 'Are you the only visitor to Jerusalem who does not know the things that have happened there in these days?' And he said to them, 'What things?' And they said to him, 'Concerning Jesus of Nazareth, a man who was a prophet mighty in deed and word before

God and all the people, and how our chief priests and rulers delivered him up to be condemned to death, and crucified him. But we had hoped that he was the one to redeem Israel. Yes, and besides all this, it is now the third day since these things happened. Moreover, some women of our company amazed us. They were at the tomb early in the morning, and when they did not find his body, they came back saying that they had even seen a vision of angels, who said that he was alive. Some of those who were with us went to the tomb and found it just as the women had said, but him they did not see.' And he said to them, 'O foolish ones, and slow of heart to believe all that the prophets have spoken! Was it not necessary that the Christ should suffer these things and enter into his glory?' And beginning with Moses and all the Prophets, he interpreted to them in all the Scriptures the things concerning himself.

So they drew near to the village to which they were going. He acted as if he were going farther, but they urged him strongly, saying, 'Stay with us, for it is towards evening and the day is now far spent.' So he went in to stay with them. When he was at table with them, he took the bread and blessed and broke it and gave it to them. And their eyes were opened, and they recognized him. And he vanished from their sight. They said to each other, 'Did not our hearts burn within us while he talked to us on the road, while he opened to us the Scriptures?' And they rose that same hour and returned to Jerusalem. And they found the eleven and those who were with them gathered together, saying, 'The Lord has risen indeed, and has appeared to Simon!' Then they told what had happened on the road, and how he was known to them in the breaking of the bread.

(Luke 24.13–35, ESV)

The word of the Lord

The word of the Lord

In conclusion

 End with the **liturgy** on p. 2 or p. 3

After the module

What have you learned from this week's module?

_____

_____

_____

_____

_____

We would love to hear your feedback on *Bread of Life* at
<www.surveymonkey.com/BreadofLife>. Your feedback
will help us to develop the course further and is really
important to us.

MODULE 4

4

Hear our prayer

Aim of this module

This module looks at the role of prayer in the Christian life, and specifically at the Lord's Prayer as the prayer of the Eucharist and as a pattern of prayer.

Way into this module

 Begin with the **liturgy** on p. 1

Watch the **video** at <www.breadoflifecourse.co.uk /lordsprayer>

The video is on the Lord's Prayer.

Main talk

Also available as a **podcast** at <www.breadoflifecourse .co.uk/maintalk4>

We pray the Lord's Prayer at almost every service in church, and this alone suggests just how important and meaningful the prayer is for us as Christians. It means so much precisely because the Lord Jesus gave it to us himself, as we read in the Gospels of Luke (11.2–4) and Matthew (6.9–13).

Let's imagine the scene. Jesus has been praying, and the disciples ask if he would teach them how to pray too. It's hardly surprising they sensed they needed help – prayer is notoriously difficult and can take a lifetime to learn!

It should be some comfort to us to know that even the disciples struggled and felt they had to be taught how to pray. We do too. In response to the disciples' request, Jesus commands them to pray in the very particular way that is so familiar to us all:

Our Father, who art in heaven,
hallowed be thy name;
thy kingdom come;
thy will be done;
on earth as it is in heaven.
Give us this day our daily bread.
And forgive us our trespasses,
as we forgive those who trespass against us.
And lead us not into temptation;
but deliver us from evil.

The Lord's Prayer is likely to be the first prayer we ever learn, and it may be the last one we remember. As Jesus gave the prayer to us, it's right to feel that it's a normal way of praying, and one to use regularly. Indeed, we could do no better than to let it become the pattern of all our prayer.

The prayer of Jesus

Jesus is our model when it comes to prayer. He prayed during his earthly ministry, not only to give us an example to follow (although that is important), but to maintain regular and intimate contact with his heavenly Father. Living in communion with his Father through this life of frequent prayer was how Jesus fulfilled his mission to us.

His experience of prayer had roots in Jesus' home life and in Jewish tradition. It's important to appreciate this, for if we don't make prayer a regular practice when our family begins to grow, it's likely to take longer for us to develop into the missionary disciples we're called to be.

The Lord's own prayer also has a more mysterious origin. Because he was the eternal Son of God, Jesus' prayer was enlivened by his relationship with God the Father *and by communion with the Holy Spirit.* As we shall see, we're invited by the Lord to address God the Father as *our* Father too. As a result, we become able to share in Jesus' relationship with the Father and the Holy Spirit.

The New Testament abounds in references to our adoption as children of God the Father: 'He destined us in love to be his sons through Jesus Christ, according to the purpose of his will, to the praise of his glorious grace which he freely bestowed on us in the Beloved' (Ephesians 1.5–6). The closeness and intimacy the Lord experienced in prayer with God the Father is open to us as well.

The life of prayer

Jesus' prayer reveals that prayer is not simply about asking God for things. As we'll see, the Lord's Prayer does express our desire for certain essentials, but ultimately God knows everything we need before we know ourselves. Prayer is really best understood as the relationship we have with God. Love between husbands and wives or between friends and family members will fail to grow if there's hardly ever any expression of affection, or if little or no time is spent together. The same is true of our relationship with God: we need to learn to spend time nurturing our relationship with him in prayer.

The structure of the Lord's Prayer

We may feel we're very familiar with the Lord's Prayer. Nonetheless, it's worth reflecting on what it is actually asking of God and of us, petition by petition, and in some detail. We can all too easily rattle off the Lord's Prayer at great speed on autopilot; stopping and thinking about it more carefully will allow our understanding to be deepened.

The prayer begins with approaching the Father's presence, first to adore him. I don't approach *my* Father but *our* Father. We're swept up into something corporate, as the prayer of the individual Christian is united to that of the wider communion of the Church.

Then there are seven petitions or requests. The first three focus on God: '*thy* name . . . *thy* kingdom . . . *thy* will'. God is the source of life and the object of our love, so it's right and proper that we place him first and not ourselves. There will be time to express our needs in the four petitions that follow.

These further four petitions ask God for what we need and draw us towards him: 'give *us* . . . forgive *us* . . . lead *us* not . . . deliver *us* . . .' Our daily bread and the forgiveness of our sins are necessary for daily life and for our growth in grace; resisting temptation and deliverance from evil are necessary for our victory over sin and death.

The petitions

- hallowed be thy name;
- thy kingdom come;
- thy will be done;
- give us this day our daily bread;
- forgive us our trespasses;
- lead us not into temptation;
- deliver us from evil.

Our Father, who art in heaven, hallowed be thy name

We begin by turning towards God our heavenly Father. We recognize, as we say 'Our Father', that God is father of us all and, as his children, we don't pray alone. Rather, we join together with the whole family of the Church in adoration of God. And we pray not only with the Church but with the Lord Jesus Christ himself, who invites us to enter into and participate in his own prayer to the Father. God is not distant but close; not only our loving parent, but also present in our midst in the Eucharist.

Thy kingdom come

Here we express our desire to enter into the kingdom of God. This is no insignificant matter! Holy Scripture tells us that the kingdom of God is a very strange place where all sorts of extraordinary things happen, such as the last becoming first and the mighty being cast down from their thrones. It's not a comfortable place, and to seek to enter it demands a leap of faith and a great degree of courage.

Thy will be done; on earth as it is in heaven

Here we say that we wish to obey the Father's will, and to follow his ways, just like those who are dwelling now in his very presence in the heavens. We recognize too that heaven is exactly where we are called to be, and that by allowing God to transform us on earth, we can now begin to live the life of heaven.

Give us this day our daily bread

We acknowledge here that it is God who sustains and provides for us, and it's striking that this is expressed in terms of bread, the most basic and staple food. But this daily bread is more than just normal bread: it is also the living bread, Christ himself, whom we receive in the Eucharist. We begin to see just how reliant we truly are on God. For the sake of our very souls, we need to be fed and nourished by Christ, to receive his very life in bread and wine. As the Lord himself says, 'Unless you eat this bread and drink this cup you have no life in you' (John 6.53, paraphrased).

Forgive us our trespasses, as we forgive those who trespass against us

If we expect others to forgive and excuse us and, indeed, if we expect God to forgive us, then we should expect to have to forgive and be generous towards others, and not to hold grudges. When we think about it, this is much harder than it sounds. We can all hold grudges and prejudices, some small and some great, and we all find certain people more difficult than others to love. But love, of course, is not an easy or 'cute' thing – it is, in fact, supremely demanding, as Jesus shows us on the cross.

And lead us not into temptation; but deliver us from evil

The temptation to sin is universal and affects us all; God has given us free will and the ability to choose to act in accordance with his will or against it. This is one of the reasons that evil is such a potent force in our world today. We follow our plea for forgiveness with an acknowledgement that we need God to help us not to sin again, to overcome temptation to resist his plans for us, to triumph over evil and to grow in grace.

The Lord's Prayer and the liturgy

Most scholars believe that the earliest written version of the Lord's Prayer is not, in fact, to be found in the Gospels, but in a collection of liturgical and teaching material called *The Didache*. Here we discover that the first Christians, those who had known the Lord and his Apostles themselves, prayed the Lord's Prayer three times a day.

St Ambrose in the fourth century and St Jerome in the fifth both wrote of the Lord's Prayer as part of the Eucharistic liturgy itself. Pope St Gregory the Great fixed it in its current position in the Eucharist for the Western Church in the sixth century. This affirmed the link between Christ's self-offering to the Father, pleaded in the Eucharistic Prayer, and the prayer of the whole community, with and in Christ, in the words of his own prayer. We still pray the

Lord's Prayer at this point after the consecration today, in the presence of Jesus himself, the one who perfectly fulfilled the Father's will. We ourselves participate in his prayer and offering, being transformed more and more into what we receive – the body of Christ.

The Lord's Prayer sums up all the prayers expressed in the liturgy and anticipates the banquet of the kingdom, of which the Eucharist is a foretaste.

The Lord's Prayer: Our way of life

We will probably come to realize before long that the implications of the Lord's Prayer are considerable! The prayer is not just a collection of common petitions, but a request from deep within us to be sustained by God. It calls us to a new way of life, a life of continual turning towards him, of reorientation. Far from being just a prayer for Sunday, to be reeled off before receiving Holy Communion, it forms the very pattern of our lives as Christians – a pattern of continual return to God the Father, who created us, to the bread of life that sustains us, to forgiveness, and to God's power to heal and protect. For good reason Tertullian, writing in the early third century, described it as 'the summary of the whole Gospel'.

The prayer is then, truly, the most trustworthy pattern for all of our prayer. Joining with the Lord in its petitions opens our hearts to his work in us and in the world, and draws us closer to him in the Eucharist, where we find the daily bread and sustenance for which we long.

Some questions to consider

If God knows what we need before we ask, why should we bother praying?

_____

_____

_____

_____

_____

What makes prayer difficult, and how can we overcome these problems?

_____

_____

_____

_____

_____

What about asking others to pray for me? Should I pray to the saints?

_____

_____

_____

_____

_____

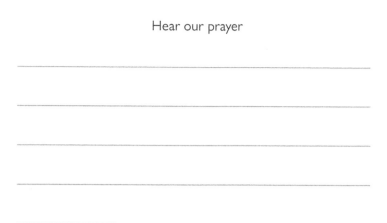 Watch the **video** at <www.breadoflifecourse.co.uk /prayerlife>

In this video, Sister Mary Angela talks about the life of prayer.

An opportunity for a group discussion. The discussion is on prayer.

Prayer

Lord Jesus Christ, Son of God, have mercy on me a sinner.
(The Jesus Prayer)

How do you think your childhood experiences have contributed to your understanding of prayer? You might like to consider early relationships that instilled in you images of God (possibly not all helpful), or patterns of prayer you followed at bedtime (perhaps God bless *X*, God bless *Y*, etc.), or saying grace at mealtimes? What impact might such experiences have had on the ways in which you pray now?

Sister Mary Angela speaks of the Lord's Prayer 'covering all possibilities – love, forgiveness, reaching out to others . . .' When do you find yourself turning to the Lord's Prayer in your private devotions? Are there other set prayers, collects or blessings you find particularly helpful, perhaps in times of need, confusion, grief or pain?

Does receiving Holy Communion feed your prayer? Is it the starting point or the end point for you?

It may be reassuring to know that Sister Mary Angela finds prayer challenging! How do you respond when your prayers seem to be met with absolute silence, and it feels as if God simply doesn't hear you?

When we're praying with others, we often use words (and expend some energy constructing sentences to express our thoughts/desires). How do you pray when there's only you and God? Do you always use words? Perhaps you silently offer people or situations on your heart? Or simply find yourself resting in God's love?

At first Sister Mary Angela thought offering healing prayer for someone required great effort on her part; she discovered that the *real* effort was of a different kind – that of emptying herself so that the Lord might use her as a channel. Can you think of times when your concern for a person or situation was so great that all you could do was surrender everything to God?

Are there phrases you cling to in impossible situations, such as 'Underneath are the everlasting arms', 'Jesus is Lord', 'God is love' and so on?

Have there been occasions when you've relied on other people to pray for you, or prayed for others who could not pray themselves? What were the circumstances?

Sister Mary Angela talks of times in the ministry of healing when 'something happens' that is beyond our language to explain. How do you respond to the mystery surrounding prayer? Perhaps you've experienced extraordinary 'coincidences' when you've been praying for others, or discovered that an action you've taken has resonated greatly with another person?

When did you last feel urged by the Holy Spirit to do something? It might have been as simple as smiling at a weary passer-by in the street!

In conclusion

Listen to the **podcast** at <www.breadoflifecourse.co.uk /interview>

The podcast is a fuller version of the interview with Sr Mary Angela that you watched earlier in the video.

 End with the **liturgy** on p. 2 or p. 3

After the module

What have you learned from this week's module?

_____

_____

_____

_____

_____

We would love to hear your feedback on *Bread of Life* at <www.surveymonkey.com/BreadofLife>. Your feedback will help us to develop the course further and is really important to us.

MODULE 5

5

The body of Christ

Aim of this module

This module looks at what it means to receive Christ in the Eucharist.

Way into this module

 Begin with the **liturgy** on p. 1

Watch the **video** at <www.breadoflifecourse.co.uk/montage>

The video is a montage of images of the body of Christ.

Main talk

((ꞯ)) Also available as a **podcast** at <www.breadoflifecourse
.co.uk/maintalk5>

Christ the Bread of Life

The God who feeds his people

The Old Testament speaks of a God who provides for and feeds his people. In the beginning, God plants the garden of Eden with 'every tree that is pleasant to the sight and good for food (Genesis 2.9).' We read later on in the Old Testament (1 Kings 19) about the prophet Elijah, who is fleeing for his life from the murderous Queen Jezebel. Elijah lies down to sleep in a state of exhaustion and despair; suddenly, he is awoken by the touch of an angel who says to him, 'Get up and eat' (v. 7). As he looks around, Elijah finds a cake baked on hot stones and a jar of water – food to keep him going on his walk to the mountain of God.

Another profound example of God feeding and sustaining those he loves comes in the story of the long pilgrimage of the people of God, from slavery in Egypt to freedom in the Promised Land. Exodus chapter 16 vividly depicts the children of Israel in the wilderness, grumbling and longing for a return to Egypt where 'we sat by the fleshpots and ate our fill of bread' (v. 3). And so they don't perish from hunger; the Lord rains bread upon them, miraculous bread, manna from heaven! 'The Israelites ate manna for forty years, until they came to a habitable land; they ate manna, until they came to the border of the land of Canaan' (Exodus 16.35).

The real presence of Christ in the bread and cup

In chapter 6 of his Gospel, we read John's account of the Feeding of the Five Thousand, which occurs almost at the time of the Passover. A huge crowd has been following Jesus and, to test them, he asks his disciples how the people might be fed. Jesus, already knowing what he is going to do, takes five loaves of bread, gives thanks and distributes the food to the crowd. Miraculously, everyone has as much as they want to eat. The next day, as he teaches his disciples what the miracle means, Jesus says to them, 'I am the bread of life' (v. 35); 'I am the living bread that came down from heaven. Whoever eats of this bread will live for ever' (v. 51). It becomes plain that Jesus is not simply employing a figure of speech:

'Very truly, I tell you, unless you eat the flesh of the Son of Man and drink his blood, you have no life in you. Those who eat my flesh and drink my blood have eternal life, and I will raise them up at the last day.' (vv. 53–54)

John tells us that many of the disciples found this teaching difficult: they 'turned back and no longer went about with him' (v. 66).

The apostle Paul and the other Gospel writers, Mark, Matthew and Luke, each give us an account of the Last Supper, when Jesus eats with his disciples, possibly on the eve of the Passover. Each writer's version differs slightly, though the heart of the narrative is the same throughout. Here's Paul's account in his first letter to the Corinthians (11.23–26):

For I received from the Lord what I also handed on to you, that the Lord Jesus on the night when he was betrayed took a loaf of bread, and when he had given thanks, he broke it and said, 'This is my body that is for you. Do this in remembrance of me.' In the same way he took the cup also, after supper, saying, 'This cup is the new covenant in my blood. Do this, as often as you drink it, in remembrance of me.' For as often as you eat this bread and drink the cup, you proclaim the Lord's death until he comes.

Sharing Christ's life

The bread is the body of Christ; the cup (or chalice) is his blood. We find – whether we turn to the account of the Last Supper above, or to those found in the synoptic Gospels (Matthew 26.26–29; Mark 14.22–25; Luke 22.14–23), or to the bread from heaven discourse in John's Gospel (6.22–59) – that the New Testament writers agree on what Jesus taught his followers. It is that in taking, blessing, breaking and sharing the bread and the cup, they are receiving him and participating in his divine life. Paul conveys this vividly: 'The cup of blessing that we bless, is it not a sharing in the blood of Christ? The bread that we break, is it not a sharing in the body of Christ?' (1 Corinthians 10.16).

Becoming the body

The Greek word **koinonia** (κοινωνία), which is translated here as 'sharing', can also be expressed as 'communion'. Paul teaches the very new Christian community in Corinth that, as they share in the Eucharist, they are in real communion with Christ. This is why they must not treat the Eucharist as simply one more ordinary meal. They must not devalue the wonderful gift of participating in the life of Christ by dividing into groups or cliques, or by rushing ahead to join the celebration while others go hungry, or by becoming drunk (1 Corinthians 11.17–22). For to participate in the Eucharist is not only to share communion with Christ, but with everyone else who is participating: 'Because there is one bread, we who are many are one body, for we all partake of the one bread' (1 Corinthians 10.17).

It is in receiving, together, the body of Christ in the Eucharist that we become the body of Christ. St Paul's teaching has born abundant fruit across the centuries, as Christians have reflected on the relationship between the celebration of the Eucharist and what is at the heart of the life of the Church. The twentieth-century Jesuit theologian, Henri de Lubac (1896–1991) famously summed this up in his perception that 'the Eucharist makes the Church'. St Augustine, addressing those preparing to receive the consecrated elements of bread and wine, said, 'Be what you see and receive what you are.' It is no accident that the two-word Latin phrase, **Corpus Christi**, the body of Christ, can be used to denote:

- the risen and ascended, physical but now glorified body of Jesus
- the Church, the mystical body of which all the baptized are members and Christ is the head
- the Blessed Sacrament itself, the bread of life of which Christ spoke in John chapter 6.

The risen body of Christ

Let's consider for a moment the second of these definitions. The Church, which has Christ, risen, ascended, glorified as its head, includes all those who have been baptized – the living, who are part of the Church here on earth, and the vastly greater number who have died and are, as saints, already enjoying the blessings of heaven. We might wonder how it is that we become part of this mystical body when we receive the Eucharist. In everyday language, our body is a physical thing that constrains us and separates us from others. However, for the biblical writers, 'body' means much more than just 'the physical stuff of which I am made'. Rather, it represents the whole person – body, soul and spirit. In receiving the body of Christ in the Eucharist, we receive the whole person of Jesus Christ, that is, Jesus Christ who is risen from the dead, and whose body – which assumed human form at the Incarnation and is now glorified – has ceased to know the limits of space and time, but is communicable to all people in every place for all eternity. Returning briefly to John 6 and the bread of life discourse, we see that Jesus unambiguously places the resurrection and the Eucharist together: 'I am the living bread that came down from heaven. Whoever eats of this bread will live for ever' (v. 51).

The sacrament of Easter

The fellowship demonstrated by meals, which are so significant a part of the Gospel account of Christ's ministry, continue to be important for the infant Church in the days following the death and rising of Christ. The Emmaus story in Luke 24.13–32 (reference was made to this in an earlier module), perhaps the most developed of the accounts of the post-resurrection meals, is probably referred to also in the longer ending of Mark (16.12) where there occurs a further meeting between the Lord and his disciples where 'he upbraided them for their lack of faith and stubbornness, because they had not believed those who saw him after he had risen' (Mark 16.14). Just as he had eaten with them before his Passion, so beyond his death it is in the context of a meal that Jesus meets with his own. And the Lukan account of the 'debrief' of the two from the Emmaus road by the Apostles (Luke 24.33–35) is the prelude to another appearance of Jesus to them all which again includes food – the risen One in Luke 24.36–43 proves his physicality by eating in their sight:

> While in their joy they were disbelieving and still wondering, he said to them, 'Have you anything here to eat?' They gave him a piece of broiled fish, and he took it and ate in their presence.
> (vv. 41–43)

It is the true body of Christ that is present to them.

John's account after Christ's appearance to Thomas and the others also has the risen Lord preparing breakfast for the Apostles on the shore of Lake Tiberias, his actions echoing the Last Supper:

> Jesus said to them, 'Come and have breakfast.' Now none of the disciples dared to ask him, 'Who are you?' because they knew it was the Lord. Jesus came and took the bread and gave it to them, and did the same with the fish.
> (John 21.12–13)

In the context of a meal, the Lord is revealed, gloriously alive. They knew it was the Lord. It is perhaps also significant that this meal leads to the restoration of Peter, whose threefold denial of the Lord before the latter's Passion is 'absolved' by a threefold commission from the Lord to be the one who feeds the flock of Christ. The encounter with the Lord around the table leads to our healing.

So when we come to the altar, to this meal of the kingdom spread before us, it is the risen Christ, now present sacramentally in every celebration of the eucharistic meal, whom we meet

- as the disciples were gathered to him in the upper room at the Last Supper;
- as we share his sacrifice at the foot of his cross (every Mass is a re-presentation of the 'full, perfect, and sufficient sacrifice' of Calvary before the Father's face);
- as at the supper in Emmaus, where they knew him in the breaking of the bread (perhaps the oldest title we have for the Eucharist);
- as on the shore of Tiberias with the disciples, where we do not have to ask, but where we simply know the hand of the risen Lord offering bread which he makes for us his body.

It is the risen Christ who is both our host, our guest and our food from heaven. Our participation in the Eucharist encapsulates the whole of the paschal mystery: the Lord's saving death, resurrection and Ascension are all made present in the offering of the holy sacrifice of the Mass.

Some questions to consider

Which passages in Scripture deepen your understanding of meeting Christ in the Eucharist?

_____

_____

_____

_____

_____

How have you experienced *koinonia* (communion) with your brothers and sisters in the Church?

_____

_____

_____

_____

_____

When has the Eucharist felt for you like a glimpse of heaven?

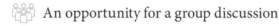 An opportunity for a group discussion

The discussion is on hymnody (the singing or composition of hymns), and how, as the author explains below, these 'may deepen our appreciation, and our living of, the sacramental life of the Church'.

Hymnody

St Augustine of Hippo once said, 'The one who sings prays twice.' Songs of praise, devotional songs in which we offer our adoration to God, are a form of prayer, expressing our attitude to God and his purposes in our lives. Emotional, poetic and spiritual, sung together hymns have the effect of unifying a congregation, creating an offering to God with one voice and one heart (see Romans 15.6). Grounded in Scripture and tradition, hymns express Christian belief, and are a means of 'absorbing' the faith.

I have chosen three quite traditional hymns which may deepen our appreciation, and our living of, the sacramental life of the Church, a starting point for discussion of what we might learn from them about the Eucharist itself.

Alleluia! sing to Jesus!

Alleluia! sing to Jesus! / His the sceptre, His the throne.
Alleluia! His the triumph, / His the victory alone.
Hark! the songs of peaceful Zion / thunder like a mighty flood.
Jesus out of every nation / has redeemed us by His blood.

Alleluia! not as orphans / are we left in sorrow now;
Alleluia! He is near us, / faith believes, nor questions how;
Though the cloud from sight received Him / when the forty days were o'er
shall our hearts forget His promise, / 'I am with you evermore'?

Alleluia! bread of angels, / Thou on earth our food, our stay;
Alleluia! here the sinful / flee to Thee from day to day:
intercessor, friend of sinners, / Earth's Redeemer, plead for me,
where the songs of all the sinless / sweep across the crystal sea.

Alleluia! King eternal, / Thee the Lord of lords we
  own;
Alleluia! born of Mary, / Earth Thy footstool, Heav'n
  Thy throne:
Thou within the veil hast entered, / Robed in flesh,
  our great high priest;
Thou on earth both priest and victim / in the
  Eucharistic feast.

This glorious hymn uses quite explicit eucharistic themes
and language. Unusually among nineteenth-century hymn
writers, its author, William Chatterton Dix (1837–98), was
a layman, active as a businessman in Bristol. Dix attended
St Raphael's Church and sang in its large choir. The church
was well known for its music and, at the time, considered
quite advanced in its Catholic style of worship. It had its
own hymn book, to which Dix contributed, but his compo-
sitions found wider audiences when they appeared in
hymnals for more general Anglican use. Dix wrote 'Alleluia!
sing to Jesus!' in 1866 during a time when he was very ill
and confined to bed for some months.

Ascended Lord (v. 2)

The Ascension of the Lord celebrates the return of the risen
Christ to his Father's glory in heaven, victorious over sin
and death, redemption won. Like the apostles, we are left
gazing into heaven, and our first response may be sadness or
loneliness, even abandonment. Dix's hymn encourages us by
reminding us that Christ does not leave us 'as orphans'. But
rather he remains with us as he has promised, interceding

for us with the Father. He is the Church's ascended Lord, but also its ever-present priestly King.

Bread of angels (v. 3)

The hymn reminds us that, like God feeding the children of Israel with heavenly manna (that miraculous food as they journeyed in the wilderness towards the Promised Land), so Jesus promises to sustain his pilgrim Church with the 'bread of angels' (a name reminding us of the manna from heaven), the Eucharist, the sacrament of the Lord's body, given to be 'on earth, our food and stay' (see John 6.48–51).

Priest and victim (v. 4)

Jesus Christ is King, but also the Saviour who 'redeemed us by His blood'. He offered himself as the acceptable sacrifice to the Father which, as it were, buys us back (redeems us) and restores what sin has spoilt. Jesus returns to heaven as ascended Lord, but also as high priest. The task of the Jewish high priest (to which Jesus's priestly work is likened) was to enter the inner sanctuary of the Temple (the Holy of Holies) where God's glory dwelt, particularly on the Day of Atonement, to offer sacrifice and make intercession for the people. Unlike that high priest, Jesus is God-made-man – 'King eternal' but also 'born of Mary'. Jesus is the sacrifice offered, and also the high priest who makes the offering of his body and blood, once, and once only, by his death on the cross. In the Eucharistic feast left to his Church, Jesus shows himself both as its priest (the one who really offers the sacrifice, the heavenly priest 'standing behind' the earthly priest at the altar) and its victim (the sacrifice of himself given to us in the bread we break and the cup we drink).

'We are an Easter people, and Alleluya is our song' (St Augustine) (v. 4)

Jesus feeds and nourishes us here, and ever lives to plead our cause. In every need we turn to him, as compassionate friend, intercessor and Redeemer, ever true to his promise: 'I am with you evermore.' The tune often used for this hymn has the name *Hyfrydol*, which means 'Good cheer'. The Eucharist is sign of the Church's optimism and confidence, as well as pledge of future joy, when we shall see the Lord on his throne of glory, our Alleluia added to the victory song of God's saints.

'Sweet Sacrament divine'

The author of this hymn was Father Francis Stanfield (1835–1914). Stanfield wrote a number of hymns to support his principal work conducting missions and retreats. Penned by one who wished to encourage believers, his words may be considered overly sentimental by some, yet possess a deep fervour. Stanfield passionately encourages the acknowledgement of Christ's presence in the Eucharist. Lord Halifax, Chairman of the English Church Union, wrote in 1930:

> On looking back over the last 75 years I see the best of all good gifts, the gifts of the Holy Communion. Our Lord's Presence in his Sacrament has been the

support, the strength and joy of my life. Without it my life would have been such as I tremble to think of, and it is because of all the Blessed Sacrament has been to me that I wish to thank God for it in the most public manner I can.

Echoing Halifax's sentiments, the hymn speaks eloquently of the many gifts offered in the Most Holy Sacrament of the Altar.

> Sweet Sacrament divine, / hid in thine earthly
>   home;
> lo! round thy lowly shrine, / with suppliant hearts we
>   come;
> Jesu, to thee our voice we raise / in songs of love and
>   heartfelt praise
> Sweet Sacrament divine.
>
> Sweet Sacrament of peace, / dear home for every
>   heart,
> where restless yearnings cease, / and sorrows all
>   depart.
> There in thine ear all trustfully, / we tell our tale of
>   misery,
> Sweet Sacrament of peace.
>
> Sweet Sacrament of rest, / ark from the ocean's
>   roar,
> within thy shelter blest / soon may we reach the
>   shore;

save us, for still the tempest raves, / save, lest we sink
   beneath the waves:
Sweet Sacrament of rest.

Sweet Sacrament divine, / earth's light and jubilee,
in thy far depths doth shine / the Godhead's majesty;
sweet light, so shine on us, we pray / that earthly joys
   may fade away:
Sweet Sacrament divine.

The background to the hymn is the story of Jesus calming
the storm (and that of Jesus walking on the water and Peter's
impulsive reaction) – love and faith weakened by doubt.
The gift of faith, and the deepening of one's trust in Jesus,
are central to the story and the hymn. We must keep our
eyes on Jesus, for salvation with him is assured. The Blessed
Sacrament of the Eucharist is the vessel Jesus has provided
for the Church to carry us through life's storms (the hostile
forces of the world) to safety. Jesus is himself that vessel, its
captain, its pilot and the light which reassuringly warms
those it carries to the far shore, our ultimate place of shelter
and sanctuary, our heavenly homeland.

Sweet Sacrament divine (v. 1)

In the Blessed Sacrament, present on the altar – whether
kneeling in adoration at the service of Benediction or, at
the Eucharist, having just received Holy Communion – we
have a gift of divine origin. A sacrament is a promise, 'an
outward and visible sign of an inward and invisible grace'
(St Augustine). Jesus is present to us in an 'earthly home',

the substance of bread which is his 'lowly shrine'. We come in prayer with hearts overflowing with many needs, yet the starting point of prayer is always adoration – 'songs of love and heartfelt praise' – as we recognize we are truly in the presence of the One whom those disciples in the boat acknowledged as Son of God.

Sweet Sacrament of peace (v. 2)

In the sacrament laid before us, we recognize the same Lord who stilled the wind and waves and brought peace, and that he can calm all anxieties now. He brings us peace as, through this Blessed Sacrament, he makes his home in us. Like the billowing waves, restless needs present in our hearts are stilled, and we can see an end to the sadness of life that threatens to drag us to the depths. The Lord is here with us, listening to fearful pleas which in hushed tones we share with him, like the beloved disciple lying close to his breast at the Last Supper. The source of our peace is here.

Sweet Sacrament of rest (v. 3)

After the storm in the Gospel story, there was calm because of the abiding presence of the Lord. Elsewhere in Scripture we read of the ark which Noah built to preserve his family and carry them to safety. In this Blessed Sacrament, the Lord provides us with a lifeboat to rescue us from the flood that threatens us continually. It is our 'ark', shelter given by God's grace and not made with our hands, but fashioned from the Lord's own body. It will bring us to the shore that will be our salvation, though, like Peter, we fear the wind and waves that threaten to overwhelm us. Like Peter we may be tempted to cry, 'Lord, save me!' (cf. Matthew 14.30). But Christ is with us and never leaves us: in this sweet Sacrament of rest his outstretched hand grasps hold of us, reassures and bears us up.

Sweet Sacrament divine (v. 4)

Beneath the outward form of the Blessed Sacrament we recognize the divine promise hidden. It is a beacon of 'light' in a darkened world. And it is a sign of 'jubilee' – the biblical jubilee year was a time of release from slavery and the remission of debts (which are our sins). Deep within this sacramental gift shines the presence of God's own inexpressible nature, his 'majesty', which is at the heart of Jesus himself and in whom 'the whole fullness of deity dwells bodily' (Colossians 2.9). We know Jesus as the true light which enlightens everyone, and which 'shines in the darkness, and the darkness has not overcome it' (John 1.5). The joy of that light makes all human joys fade and we are possessed only by Jesus who is and will be our heavenly joy.

Soul of my Saviour

Soul of my Saviour, sanctify my breast,
Body of Christ, be Thou my saving guest,
Blood of my Saviour, bathe me in Thy tide,
Wash me with water flowing from Thy side.

Strength and protection may Thy Passion be,
O blessed Jesus, hear and answer me;
Deep in Thy wounds, Lord, hide and shelter me,
So shall I never, never part from Thee.

Guard and defend me from the foe malign,
In death's dread moments make me only Thine;
Call me and bid me come to Thee on high,
Where I may praise Thee with Thy saints for ay.

This little hymn speaks of the grace that flows from partaking of the body and blood of the Lord, reaching beyond the physical elements of this sacramental food to the Lord's very soul and divinity. Based on a Latin prayer, 'Anima Christi', dating from the early fourteenth century, an English translation of the prayer in hymn form became popular in the latter half of the nineteenth century in British Roman Catholic churches (often used for evening services of Benediction of the Blessed Sacrament, a devotional service where the Eucharistic host is exposed on the altar, venerated with incense, hymns and prayers, and used to give a blessing over the people; the same tradition has been adopted in a number of Anglican churches). Its use at the Eucharist as a thanksgiving after Holy Communion has become popular, and the words appear in a number of quite mainstream Anglican hymnals.

Sacred wounds

Devotion to the wounds of the crucified Lord has been a part of Christian devotion since earliest times. On Calvary, the Lord's hands and feet were pierced and his side pierced by the soldier's spear; these wounds are not majored on in the crucifixion narratives, but they are crucial to several resurrection appearances of Jesus – the reality of the wounds, the ability to see them and even place fingers in them, is impressed upon the apostles by the risen Christ as a necessary part of their belief in the truth of his risen body (John 20:20, 21). Thomas, not present on that occasion, says he will not believe unless he touches these wounds. When Jesus appears to him, he encourages Thomas to do what he desires as a guarantee that his risen body is one with the body that suffered on the cross (John 20: 24–29). It is not said that Thomas did this, but his reaction to Jesus' bidding was the cry of utter belief, 'My Lord and my God!' (John 24.28).

Healing wounds

Echoing the image of the Suffering Servant in Isaiah 53, St Peter writes of Christ that 'He himself bore our sins in his body on the tree, that we might die to sin and live to righteousness. By his wounds you have been healed' (1 Peter 2.24). St Bernard (d. 1153) popularized a spirituality based on the humanity of Jesus and his Passion; and St Francis of Assisi (d. 1226) and his attested receiving of the marks of the Lord's Passion (the stigmata) contributed to this tradition. Julian of Norwich, who in 1373 during a severe illness received sixteen revelations ('shewings') of the crucified Christ, later wrote after contemplating this experience for many years:

> I saw the red blood trickle down from under the garland, hot and fresh and plentiful, as it did at the time of his Passion when the crown of thorns was pressed into his blessed head – he who was both God and man and who suffered for me . . . And while I saw the blood flow from his head I never ceased from saying, 'Blessed be the Lord.'

(Revelations of Divine Love 4, 8)

Alongside this, theologians looked to the wound in the Lord's side from which issued blood and water (John 19.34), as referring to the waters of baptism and also the Precious Blood of the eucharistic cup.

Soul of my Saviour, sanctify my breast (v. 1)

Singing this hymn, we may have just received the body and blood of our Lord Jesus, that Holy Communion where he invites us to sit at his table and eat, promises to make his home with us and abide always, entering into us so that his divine life may be ours. This is the promise of the Eucharist. Every communion allows his life to be renewed in us so, by his grace, we may become more like him. This communion with Jesus becomes a process of sanctification, his life increasing in us, so that our souls and bodies become a living sacrifice of praise. Christ, the guest who makes his home in us by our invitation, not by forcing himself on us, offers us the gift of salvation – a free gift to all who turn to him recognizing their need.

Strength and protection may Thy Passion be (v. 2)

At the Eucharist, memorial of Christ's death and Passion (the re-presentation of his sacrifice on Calvary), we stand at the foot of his cross. It is fearful and lonely only if we take our eyes off him. The battle he wages on the cross with sin and death will be the covering with which he clothes us, our strength and protection. Our prayer as we gaze on the cross is that we never be separated from Jesus, and the sure place of safety in which we have confidence is within the very wounds of his Passion, signs and tokens of his victory. On the altar of the cross the wounds of love are a sanctuary, a place of shelter, a place of rich blessing. So I can say, because I know it in reality from my place of safety hidden in his wounds:

> I am crucified with Christ. It is no longer I who live, but Christ who lives in me. And the life I now live in the flesh I live by faith in the Son of God, who loved me and gave himself for me.
> (Galatians 2.20)

Guard and defend me from the foe malign (v. 3)

St Peter tells how in our Christian lives we must be watchful because our 'adversary the devil prowls around like a roaring lion, seeking someone to devour' (1 Peter 5.8). This is the foe malign, our malicious enemy. We have placed our hope in the light which is Christ and not in the one who offers only the darkness of death. At our passing from this world we pray that we may hear the strong call of the Lord Jesus Christ who has already won the victory over sin and death. St Richard of Chichester, dying in the year 1253, called for a crucifix. Gazing on it, he prayed: 'Thanks be to thee, my Lord Jesus Christ, for all the benefits thou hast given me, for all the pains and insults thou hast borne for me.' Mindful of this, perhaps we might pray that we may glorify God, saying with the apostle Paul: 'Thanks be to God, who gives us the victory through our Lord Jesus Christ' (1 Corinthians 15.57).

🎙 Listen to the **podcast** at <www.breadoflifecourse.co.uk
/max-barley>

In this podcast, Max Barley talks about how choral music
and hymns can strengthen our faith.

In conclusion

 End with the **liturgy** on p. 2 or p. 3

After the module

What have you learned from this week's module?

_____

_____

_____

_____

_____

We would love to hear your feedback on *Bread of Life* at
<www.surveymonkey.com/BreadofLife>. Your feedback
will help us to develop the course further and is really
important to us.

MODULE 6

6

Go in peace to love and serve the Lord

Aim of this module

This module explains why the eucharistic life is missional and outward looking.

Way into this module

 Begin with the **liturgy** on p. 1

⊞ Watch the **video** at <www.breadoflifecourse.co.uk /discussion>

The video shows several people talking about what the Eucharist means to them.

Main talk

((◌)) Also available as a **podcast** at <www.breadoflifecourse .co.uk/maintalk6>

The door

If my house were to catch fire and I had time to rescue just two objects, what would I save? That's a question I sometimes ask myself because it is an interesting way of working out what is most precious to me.

My first object would be a beautiful sixth-century crucifix that a friend bought me when I was made a bishop and which would slip conveniently into a pocket. The second object I would rescue is a rather less practical one because it would be my pool table and I'm not sure quite how I would carry it!

What if you were to apply the same question to your church building? What if it caught fire one night and you could rescue only two things? In other words what are the single two most important objects in your church?

The first would be the Blessed Sacrament because in the consecrated host Jesus is fully and physically present. That little wafer of bread is the most precious thing in all this world, more valuable than all the gold, silver and precious gems on the planet. But what would you collect as the second object? That is rather more complex. A chalice? A rich vestment? The curate? I think the thing I would rescue second would be the door. For me, after the Blessed Sacrament, the door is the most precious object in the church. Why? Because the most important thing we do in the Mass is to walk through that door and go home again.

Being called and being sent

In Mark 3.14 Jesus called the twelve, 'To be with him, and to be sent out'. That is just one single phrase with no full stop because to be with Jesus and to be sent by him is one single action. In the Mass we make time to be *with* Jesus. We meet him in the words of Scripture and in the bread and wine of the Eucharist. But then in the very same action Jesus sends us out like the disciples to share his kingdom love with others.

It's all in the name. The word 'Mass' comes from the Latin *missa* which means 'sent' so that in the Latin the priest says at the end, '*Ite missa est*.' The same Latin verb is found buried in the word 'disMISSAl' which is the name we give to the very final words in the Mass. And the same verb is found again in the word 'MISSion' which is the term we give to God's whole action in loving the world back to life in his Son Jesus Christ who was sent into the world to save us. So from the **Mass**, we are **sent** to share in God's **mission**.

We don't go to Mass simply for our own well-being. We don't go so that we ourselves can be saved or know Jesus more closely. That would be pure self-indulgence. No, we go to Mass for the benefit of the world. We are thrown out through the doors in order to share in God's mission. We are sent to share our faith with others.

The problem is that a lot of people get very nervous when it comes to the business of sharing their faith. They assume it will be cringey and embarrassing, involving for example standing on street corners wearing a sandwich board emblazoned with 'Jesus saves'.

Actually, faith-sharing should be every bit as natural and easy as praying. And in fact, the elements of the Mass that we have studied in this course show us just how we can share our faith in our everyday lives.

Prayer

The Mass is one prayer. Yes, it incorporates intercession, in which we offer specific intentions to God, but every word that is breathed from the Invocation of the Trinity to the Dismissal is a prayer because it is offered to God.

As those sent from the altar to share the good news of Jesus with others, the first thing we should be doing is praying. All of us know people who are not yet Christians and who, in their hearts, are longing for the fresh start and the new life that only knowing Jesus can bring. So think of five people who are known well to you and get praying for them that they might come to know Jesus in the Mass for themselves.

It may be a family member. It may be one of your own children who has drifted away from church despite a Christian upbringing. It may be a colleague from work or a friend from a sports team. It may be the person who serves you in the supermarket. Whoever they are, pray for each of your five every single day by name. If you do that, you can be absolutely sure that an opportunity will arise to speak to one of the five about your faith. Faith-sharing begins with prayer.

Invitation

In Luke 14.21, a landowner sends his servant out into the streets and lanes to invite to his banquet, 'the poor, the crippled, the blind, and the lame'. To the banquet of the Mass God invites us all.

As those who have been invited to that banquet, we are sent by Jesus to invite others. In other words, that servant is you. There is no greater gift you can ever offer another human being than inviting them to the banquet of eternal life which we call the Mass.

Many people get very nervous about having to put their faith into words. They think they don't know enough or won't be able to answer the clever questions they may be asked. But anyone can invite.

If you are praying for five friends, intentionally seek out an opportunity to invite one of them to church for a Sunday Mass. The worst they can say is no, and even if it's a no they will be pleased to have been invited. And many will say yes.

If you don't feel ready to invite someone to Mass, then what about finding or organizing a church social event they might enjoy? It is very easy to introduce a simple mission element, simply by providing someone with an opportunity to tell their story of faith.

Many people presume that church is a private place for a small group of people and they won't be welcome. Many are terrified of simply stepping through the doors. Those people won't just turn up! They need to be invited. And what a gift that invitation is! The doors you are throwing open allow entry to nothing less than the banquet of eternity.

So whom are you going to invite?

Proclamation

In the Mass, the word of God is proclaimed to us. Especially in the Gospels, Jesus puts the kingdom of God into words and invites us to participate in it. Yes, he lived the gospel through his deeds. But he also spoke the gospel and called people to respond.

As those who come to be with Jesus to hear the word proclaimed, we are sent to speak that word to others. St Peter writes in his first letter, 'Always be ready to make your defence to anyone who demands from you an account of the hope that is in you' (3.15). If we pray and if we invite, the time will surely come when somebody or other will want us to speak about what it is that we believe.

You don't need to be a theologian to put your faith into words. You don't even need to be clever. You just need to be authentic.

Try to think through your answers to some of these questions. How did you become a Christian in the first place? What would your life be like without Jesus? What is precious to you about being part of the Church? How have you been able to go on believing during the hard times in your life? What words would you use to describe Jesus? If you can answer these questions, you can share your faith.

And of course, if someone asks you about faith, you don't need to give a great long sermon! In fact, the most important thing you can do is listen to them.

Generosity

In the Mass, we encounter the astonishing, breathtaking generosity of the God who gives us all things. We are ordinary, sinful, mortal beings, yet God raises us up and feeds us with the very life of his Son. Through the sacrificial generosity of Jesus' death on the cross, he forgives us, sets us free and saves us from death. He gives us gifts with which to serve him and the assurance of his constant love and companionship. And he gives us all this, even though we have done nothing at all to deserve it.

As those who experience the generosity of God in the Mass, we are sent to be generous ourselves. The generosity to which God calls us is not the grudging, half-hearted generosity of the world which always wants to know what it will get in return. Our generosity should be free, boundless and unconditional.

Yes, there will be occasions when we are called to put faith into words. But what makes us stand out in the crowd is not the words that we speak but our lifestyles. It is when we put faith into practice that people sit up and take notice.

When a new neighbour moves into the street, why not take them a tray of cakes? When you're at work, why not be the first person to offer to make others tea and coffee? When someone asks you to donate to charity, why not give sacrificially? When you're on a train and the trolley comes past, why not offer to buy your neighbour a coffee? When you're in a café or restaurant, why not look the waiter in the eye and thank them for looking after you?

In all these simple ways and in so many others, we are pointing to the generosity of God. People will observe what we are doing and wonder why.

Justice

In the Mass we see the world as it should be. The kingdom is anticipated and we share together in the life of heaven, perceiving for a while that new Jerusalem described by Isaiah, where all share in a banquet of fine wines and rich food. In the Eucharist all are equal, all have a place, all are fed, all are precious and all are honoured.

In the Mass, we participate for a while in the justice of the kingdom, and so from the Mass we are sent to build a world that reflects something of the justice of God. It is impossible to share in the Mass and then look on and do nothing when children go hungry, when the homeless lie in the streets, when family life is torn apart by debt or when injustice is allowed to endure. It is no wonder that Christians who love

Jesus in the Eucharist have always been at the forefront of the struggle for justice and reconciliation.

Our participation in the Mass will inevitably express itself as we make a stand for justice. That will mean we are generous to those who support the poor and to those who suffer or are in pain. It may mean that we volunteer for charity work or social projects. It may mean that our local church runs groups and organizations that meet the needs we encounter in the communities we serve. It will most certainly mean that we do all we can to protect the environment and work for the sustainability of creation.

As we make a stand for justice, we are putting our faith into practice and sharing in God's mission of bringing life, love and hope into the world.

RUN into the world!

The Dismissal can be such a furtive and understated part of the Mass. 'Go in peace to love and serve the Lord,' says the priest. 'In the name of Christ. Amen,' mutter the people and then shuffle off for a cup of weak coffee. It should be so much more than that! This is the consummation of the whole Eucharist! We should shout these words and then go to transform our homes and communities in the love of Christ.

I was recently celebrating the Mass for a group of primary school children and I told them, once they had said 'Go in peace to love and serve the Lord', to run out the room as fast as they could. It was fabulous chaos! The moment the words were spoken, there was an almighty scramble for the door, the children finally escaped and then ran as fast as their legs could carry them across the field, shouting as loudly as they could, 'Jesus is risen!'

Now, there is a proper Dismissal! From the altar where we meet Christ, we run to share Christ that all might know the perfect joy of the banquet of eternity.

Some questions to consider

Can you think of three or four ways in which you can share your faith with others?

_____

_____

_____

_____

_____

What makes you nervous about sharing your faith?

_____

_____

_____

_____

Go in peace to love and serve the Lord

Can you think of some better words for the Dismissal at the end of the Mass?

_____

_____

_____

_____

_____

In conclusion

 Watch the **video** at <www.breadoflifecourse.co.uk /closing>

The closing video for the *Bread of Life* course takes place back in Jerusalem.

 End with the **liturgy** on p. 2 or p. 3

After the module

What have you learned from this week's module?

_____

_____

_____

_____

_____

We would love to hear your feedback on *Bread of Life* at <www.surveymonkey.com/BreadofLife>. Your feedback will help us to develop the course further and is really important to us.

Acknowledgments

Bread of Life was made possible through a large investment of money and resources from both the Confraternity of the Blessed Sacrament and SPCK. In February 2018, Bishop Philip North connected the two organizations and suggested that there was an opportunity to create something special that would help people discover more about Jesus Christ.

As the two organizations met, an idea started to form of a course that would build out over time. Written by the best theological thinkers and partnered with tools and resources to enable anyone to teach the material, it would help people enter a deeper relationship with their faith in Christ.

It has been a privilege to chair the Editorial Board and I'm grateful to every member for their dedication, prayer, and support.

I would like to thank Fr Dominic Cyrus, Fr Ron Farrell, Deacon Sarah Gillard-Faulkner, Fr Ed Morrison and Fr Adam Wogan, along with the staff of the CBS, ACS and Church Union – Fr Adam Edwards, Fr Darren Smith, Robert Jordan and Mary Bashford – who have provided such valuable help with admin, PR advice and meeting space.

I am grateful most of all to those who have contributed written, recorded and video material – Bishop Roger, Fr Ron Farrell, Fr Ed Morrison, Fr Philip Barnes, Fr Chris Trundle, Bishop Jonathan Baker, Bishop Philip North, Sr

Acknowledgments

Mary Angela, Joan Whyman, Max Barley, Liquona and the filming team in Jerusalem, Boogaloo Media, and Parvis Magna Productions Ltd.

Special thanks must go to the team at SPCK who have spent countless hours producing, designing and project managing this course – Sam Richardson, Primavera Quantrill, Mark Read, Chris Hawtin, Alison Barr and Rima Devereaux.

Most importantly, I would like to express my appreciation to Bishop Roger Jupp for his insight, prayer, dedication and passion for the project. He has empowered and led us to this point. Without his gentle guidance, *Bread of Life* would have faltered in its early days. His love for Christ and for us (unlike its Chair's!) has known no irritation or frustration, only patience and kindness. We are forever in his debt.

Finally, thanks must go to my wife and son – Catherine and Edmund – who have been there in the frustrations and in the joys, who have daily reminded me of the deep love of God, and without whom I would not be able to carry out God's work in the world.

Fr. Matthew Cashmore SSC
Chair of the Editorial Board, *Bread of Life*

A final acknowledgement comes from Bishop Roger Jupp on behalf of the Confraternity of the Blessed Sacrament.

The late **Laurence Roy De Thier** left a very generous bequest to CBS on his death in 2013. It was made in memory of his father, **Laurence William De Thier**, who had had died in 1968. His son asked that this should be used, at the discretion of the Confraternity, specifically 'for the purpose of the advancement of the Catholic faith in the Anglican Tradition.' It is this gift which has helped finance the *Bread of Life* project. As we record this generosity, and celebrate the memory of both father and son as we ought in prayer, we trust that the purpose to which we have devoted this benefaction will fulfil this intention. Having once received the Lord faithfully in the Blessed Sacrament during their pilgrimage on earth, now in the nearer presence of the Lord they behold Him face to face. *Ut requiescant in pace.*

Sources and copyright acknowledgements

Every effort has been made to acknowledge fully the sources of material reproduced in this book. The publisher apologizes for any omissions that may remain and, if notified, will ensure that full acknowledgements are made in a subsequent edition.

Bread of life liturgies

At the beginning of a module: 'Lord Jesus Christ, in the most wonderful Sacrament of the Eucharist': Fr Ron Farrell's free translation of the traditional Collect for Corpus Christ/Thanksgiving for Holy Communion.

At the end of a module: 'Support us, O Lord, all the day long': prayer by John Henry Newman, in the public domain.

At the end of a module: 'The bread you give, O God': lightly edited and taken from *Opening Prayers: Collects in contemporary language* (Canterbury Press, 2001) but originally prepared for *The Sacramentary, Volume 1: Sundays and Feasts* (© International Commission on English in the Liturgy, 1977).

Bible acknowledgements

Modules 1 and 2: ESV

Module 3: esv, kjv, niv, nrsv
Module 4: rsv
Module 5: main talk nrsv, hymnody esv
Module 6: nrsv

Other sources

Extracts from The Book of Common Prayer, the rights in which are vested in the Crown, are reproduced by permission of the Crown's Patentee, Cambridge University Press.

Common Worship:

'Take and eat': Words at the Giving of Communion, <http://justus.anglican.org/~ss/commonworship/hc/wordsgiving.html>

'Christ is our peace': Introductions to the Peace, <http://justus.anglican.org/~ss/commonworship/hc/intropeace.html>

'Go in peace': Christ is our Peace, <https://www.churchofengland.org/prayer-and-worship/worship-texts-and-resources/common-worship/common-material/new-patterns-16>

Extracts from *Common Worship: Services and Prayers* are copyright © The Archbishops' Council, 2000, and are reproduced by permission. All rights reserved. <copyright@churchofengland.org>

Support networks related to the *Absolute Truth* video

If you have been a victim of crime
<www.victimsupport.org.uk>
<www.gov.uk/get-support-as-a-victim-of-crime>
<www.report-it.org.uk/organisations_that_can_help>
<www.catch-22.org.uk/victims>
<www.supportline.org.uk/problems/victim-support/

Restorative justice
<restorativejustice.org.uk>
<https://why-me.org>
<www.remediuk.org>

Christian organizations that support those in and post custody
<prisonfellowship.org.uk>
<www.message.org.uk/prisons-and-enterprise/>
<www.christianprisonresourcing.org.uk/our-vision/>
<daylightcpt.org>
<www.prisonadvice.org.uk/parish-support>

THE CONFRATERNITY OF
THE BLESSED SACRAMENT

Registered Charity No. 1082897

Application for Admission
and Gift Aid Declaration

The Objects and Rules are set out on the back of the
Quarterly Paper. The Confraternity accepts the principles
of Forward in Faith's Agreed Statement on Communion

I,   being a communicant member of the Church of England
or of another Church approved by the Council-General, accepting the catholic faith and
observing the practices of the catholic religion, hereby declare my full agreement with the
Objects and accept the Rules of the Confraternity of the Blessed Sacrament, and ask to be
admitted as an Associate.

Please cross through the following paragraph if this does not apply to you
* I am a UK taxpayer and understand that if I pay less Income Tax and/or Capital Gains Tax
in the current tax year than the amount of Gift Aid claimed on all my donations it is my
responsibility to pay any difference.

Signature   Date

Address (*including postcode*)

E-Mail   Telephone   Ward

I,   being an existing CBS Associate attached to the Ward,
do from personal knowledge and after due enquiry recommend the aforesaid applicant to
be admitted as an Associate.
Signature   Date

The Enrolment Fee is £10 which includes the manual and medal. Thereafter on the
anniversary of enrolment it will be £6 per annum. Alternatively Life Membership is £60.
Lapel Badges, replacement Medals and Manuals at a cost of £2 each are available from Mrs
Mary Bashford at the address below.

Please return this form to:
Mrs Mary Bashford (CBS), 16 Commercial Street, Birmingham B1 1RS

THE CONFRATERNITY OF THE BLESSED SACRAMENT

Registered Charity No. 1082897

Application for Admission and Gift Aid Declaration

The Objects and Rules are set out on the back of the Quarterly Paper. The Confraternity accepts the principles of Forward in Faith's Agreed Statement on Communion

---

I,   being a priest of the catholic Church in communion with the Church of England or of another Church approved by the Council-General, accepting the catholic faith and observing the practices of the catholic religion, hereby declare my full agreement with the Objects and accept the Rules of the Confraternity of the Blessed Sacrament, and ask to be admitted as an Associate.

Please cross through the following paragraph if this does not apply to you
* I am a UK taxpayer and understand that if I pay less Income Tax and/or Capital Gains Tax in the current tax year than the amount of Gift Aid claimed on all my donations it is my responsibility to pay any difference.

Signature   Date

Address (*including postcode*)

E-Mail   Telephone   Ward

I,   being an existing CBS Associate attached to the Ward, do from personal knowledge and after due enquiry recommend the aforesaid applicant to be admitted as an Associate.
Signature   Date

The Enrolment Fee is £10 which includes the manual and medal. Thereafter on the anniversary of enrolment it will be £6 per annum. Alternatively Life Membership is £60. Lapel Badges, replacement Medals and Manuals at a cost of £2 each are available from Mrs Mary Bashford at the address below.

Please return this form to:
Mrs Mary Bashford (CBS), 16 Commercial Street, Birmingham B1 1RS